The Dialogues of
Archibald MacLeish
and Mark Van Doren

Mark Van Doren and Archibald MacLeish

The Dialogues of Archibald MacLeish and Mark Van Doren

EDITED BY
WARREN V. BUSH

NEW YORK ⇒ E. P. DUTTON & CO., INC. ⇒ 1964

FOR *Drea* AND *Kit*

CONTENTS ≥ ≥ ≥

As a television producer for CBS News I report on the works and lives of men. The works of men often speak plainly for themselves. Their lives do not.

Therefore to do my job I must constantly seek out styles and techniques which will provide deeper, more rewarding insights into contemporary men of consequence.

But even with acceptable techniques at hand, something else is required before a man—any man—will step aside and invite a stranger into his life.

"I hope you don't think the idea is presumptuous," I said.

"Not in the least," Archibald MacLeish replied. "I think the basic idea is sound. And it also has a certain fascination for me, but I'd like to think about it."

"It might be better if we got together and discussed it more fully."

"Well, I'll be leaving Conway in a few days. I'm going to Washington for the Malraux dinner, and then I'll be in Europe for a while."

"Could we get together in Washington?"

"That might be possible."

"All right," I said, "I'll try to see you there." We hung up. Later we met in Washington.

"No," said MacLeish, "I haven't changed my mind about the idea. I'm just not sure it can be brought off. You know, I've been through some of these television things before, and they've never been too successful. Your production methods practically prohibit getting at things. And I'm sure Ada wouldn't take lightly to a lot of men tramping about our house with a lot of equipment."

"There won't be any of that," I replied. "I plan to use two cameramen and one soundman. That's all. There'll be no lights. No microphone, booms or cables. No tripods. No reflectors. None of the usual equipment. I've located some highly imaginative film-makers who I think can do the job. All of their equipment is self-contained and portable. It's hand-held, and goes wherever they go, or wherever you go. So nothing has to be staged."

"No lights, you say?" MacLeish mused.

"None."

"None of that great, bulky camera equipment?"

"None."

"And we can move about whenever, wherever we want?"

"Yes."

"And you can get the sound?"

"Yes. And we won't tie you down with a microphone. You won't be tied down in any way."

"Do you have some new way of getting the sound?"

"Yes. It's experimental, but I think it's worth the try."

"And we wouldn't have to start and stop all the time?"

"No. You can talk as long as you like. Or not at all. It would be up to you."

"I've never heard of such a way of doing things."

"As I said, it's experimental. But the technique and equipment have advanced to a point where I think it's worth a try. And besides, I don't think there's any other way of bringing off the concept on film."

"Wouldn't it be simpler just to use audio tape?"

"But, Mr. MacLeish," I said, "I'm a *television* producer."

"Yes, of course, that's right," he said with Scots delight.

"And I believe that seeing a man say what he wants to say, in the environment he chooses to say it in, is as important as what he says," I went on.

"In my case, seeing me might prove to be a singular distraction," MacLeish said, laughing.

"Seeing you would provide dimension to what you chose to say."

"I know a lot of my friends who would disagree with you about that," MacLeish added good-humoredly, "but let me get this whole thing clear. If I were to do this with an as yet unknown friend, there would be no restriction on what we talked about or how long we talked?"

"Correct."

"There would be no topics? No one would ask us questions?"

"No topics; no questions."

"And how long do you see this operation going on?"

"Oh, a day or two; possibly three. I think it's something we have to feel our way with."

"That could add up to quite a lot of material."

"Yes."

"And who would edit these private conversations? Who would be responsible for reducing all this material to a one-hour film?"

"I would."

"You would?"

"That's right."

"I see. Well, would I—would I and my companion in conversation—be allowed to know what you were using in the film before it was broadcast?"

"I would prefer not."

"Well, you know, a man could be made to look pretty foolish, or he could get off some things which might appear to be foolish under the circumstances you wish for making this film."

"Yes, I know."

"You do know that?"

"Yes. I know that."

MacLeish quietly considered all this, and me. Then he said, "All right. Let me think about it some more. I'll let you know when I return from Europe."

There was no waiting for his return from Europe. On the day after the alarming plunge the New York stock market took on May 28, 1962, we met in Paris at my hotel, the Elysée Park. MacLeish reminisced lengthily, with great feeling, recalling the time when he as a young man, with his wife, Ada, went off to live and write in Paris on the shaky stakes of an unforeseen stock windfall. And then came the great 1929 collapse of the stock market.

After a while, I asked him, "Did you think about it?"

"Yes, I did. But don't tell me you came all the way over here just to get my answer."

"No," I said, "I'm here to make arrangements for another film." Then I threw in: "But I think you'll agree there's no better place to arrive at decisions than here in Paris. Here there's the right consolation for a *no,* and here there's the right champagne for a *yes.*"

We laughed, and although it was breakfast, we drank champagne.

"You realize," MacLeish said, "I'm only speaking for myself. I can't speak for my friends. I can't even speak *to* them about the project. You must do that. That's your job."

"All right," I said, "but first you must tell me who your friends are, and something about those friendships."

He did that. At least he told me who some of them were. Statesmen, poets, scholars, historians, scientists, jurists, performers, sportsmen were named as friends he knew well, whom he held in great esteem, for whom he had great affection, and who, he believed, held him in the same regard.

And then, abruptly, he said: "We'll have to continue this in Conway. I'm here in Paris to spend time with my son Ken and his family. They're very much on my mind, so we shouldn't be talking about this project now. I'll be back in Conway in a week or two. It will be better there."

So we went away again.

When we met at his home in Conway, it was better. Ada was there, and he was home in his New England, and it was spring, and green.

Right off he said: "If we deliberately try to pick somebody it will be for some special reason and it won't be right. But let me suggest this: every year Ada and I visit Mark Van Doren and his wife, Dorothy, down at his home in Cornwall. We spend a few days there. And then they come and visit with Ada and me. We've done this for years. Mark is one of my oldest friends. We know each other well, and I have great respect for him. And I enjoy being with him enormously. And I would guess he feels the same way about me."

Mrs. MacLeish said: "You needn't guess about that. There's no doubt that he feels the same way about you as you do about him."

"Well," MacLeish said, "I do know I would feel much more comfortable with Mark. Any other way would be staged. It wouldn't work. Look," he continued with enthusiasm, "we could do it right here at the farm. The Van Dorens will be visiting with us about the middle of June. The girls can have an uninterrupted time together, and Mark and I can talk about all the things that we usually talk about."

"Isn't that the way it always is, Archie?" asked Mrs. MacLeish piquantly.

14

"Of course," MacLeish went on, "I can't ask Mark to do this. You must talk with him. If he doesn't want to do it, we'll have to think of something else that's just as right. Maybe there isn't any right way."

"About your equipment, Mr. Bush," Mrs. MacLeish said, "Archie has told me about it, and I want you to know I have no objections. But you will be careful, won't you?"

I assured her every care would be taken.

I telephoned Mark Van Doren from my office in New York. I briefly outlined the project, and asked for an appointment to see him, to discuss it further.

He said, "Does Archie want to do this?"

I said, "Yes."

"Well, there's no need for you to make the long trip up here to talk about it. If Archie thinks it's a good idea, and he wants to do it with me, it's fine with me."

"Then you'll do it?"

"Yes, that's what I said. As long as Archie wants me to."

"He does."

"All right," he said. "Good-bye."

On the morning of June 18, 1962, my crew and I arrived at Uphill Farm. Mark and Dorothy Van Doren had arrived the evening before. MacLeish and Van Doren, early risers, were being served breakfast on the east terrace. My two cameramen and soundman unobtrusively began their work.

At first, MacLeish and Van Doren were self-conscious. "Is

there anything in particular you want us to start talking about?" asked Van Doren. "Perhaps you want us to move someplace, to sit differently?" added MacLeish.

I gave my first and final instruction: "Gentlemen, say what you want, go wherever you want, do whatever you want, whenever you want to do it."

With no more than that, they slipped gratefully into the spirit of the project, for soon the crew found they could do their work with no more notice than is given accepted members of a household staff.

For two lengthy days MacLeish and Van Doren moved at will in and about the Uphill Farm house, now mature with carefully added ells and wings, terraces and accumulated comforts. They started off on jaunty ambles over the slopes and through the fields, through the woods. They took to the terraces as the sun and shadows allowed. They fished. They swam. And wherever they were, they talked. They spoke together as they had always done, about the things important to them. They spoke together freely and respectfully as only friends and equals can do. And in so doing, they shared an act of faith in each other with a stranger—the public, of which I was one.

In the early evening of August 2, 1962, one hour of "The Dialogues of Archibald MacLeish and Mark Van Doren" was broadcast by the CBS Television Network.

That was the way "The Dialogues" began; that was the way it might have ended—but for this book.

What follows is raw material, the stuff of spontaneity. It includes not only the dialogues used in the original broadcast but also most of the dialogues recorded during the entire filming at Uphill Farm.

Where editing has taken place, it has been carried out in the interest of smoothness of continuity; the dialogue in this Foreword, however, was reconstructed from memory.

Perhaps this more permanent document should begin as the broadcast began, with no more introduction than:

"They call each other Archie and Mark. They share much in common. They're Americans, both natives of Illinois. Both were born in the 1890's. Poets, dramatists, and scholars alike, between them they have four Pulitzer Prizes. They sit easily among their peers in the American Academy of Arts and Letters.

"Both have sunk roots in Yankee New England: Archie here at Uphill Farm in Conway, Massachusetts; Mark in Cornwall Hollow, Connecticut. They are neighbors. They are old friends.

"And when they get together they speak of many things: of the world of man, the world of nature, and sometimes of the universe next door.

"These, then, are some of 'The Dialogues of Archibald MacLeish and Mark Van Doren.'"

WARREN V. BUSH

Antigua, West Indies

PART ONE ➺ ➺ ➺

June 18, 1962

Having breakfasted, MacLeish and Van Doren are walking through the tall, drying pasture grasses of the Berkshire Hills surrounding Uphill Farm.

MacLeish

. . . As I was telling you last night, Mark, the thing that intrigues me so much as I look back on my beginnings is why in the name of God I ever wanted to be a poet, or why I thought I *could* be is an even graver question.

You take the kind of world in which you and I grew up; writers weren't held in much esteem and poets in less than none, and there was practically nobody writing verse of any interest along the time of the First World War. What is it that draws a kid so passionately toward this use of words as a material of art that nothing else will satisfy him? Why is it that he commits himself to a life which in prospect doesn't look financially very promising, and yet he will go to any lengths to pursue it? Is it because he has a peculiar view of the world that he wants to get across? I don't think so. Or is it because he has a very strong musical sense? Is that more nearly it?

VAN DOREN

That comes much closer to it, because ultimately it isn't what he says so much, although he'd better say something. More importantly what he says must be said in such a way that nobody can forget it. I would say that. I would say that any young poet started in the first place by reading poetry.

MACLEISH

Certainly that's the way you begin. Do you remember who you read?

VAN DOREN

Yes. I remember very distinctly; my favorite was Wordsworth. I was in college, a junior in college, I think, and no poetry had made any great difference to me until suddenly I found myself reading him. To myself.

MACLEISH

Did he move you musically or was it something he was saying?

VAN DOREN

No. No, it was the music. I would go into my room—I had a room on the third floor of my father's house in Urbana, Illinois—that's where the university is, you know; we lived there. I found myself going upstairs and closing the door and intoning Wordsworth to myself. I was afraid that I would be heard, you know, and I thought people wouldn't like that; and yet I did it just as loudly as I pleased and with all the intonations that seemed to be proper. It just happened that it was Wordsworth for me.

MacLeish

Well, this just indicates the immeasurable degree of your superior wisdom, because when I started out I took off from Swinburne. He's somebody I can't read now and haven't been able to read for years. But what took me, I feel sure, was the music. It was some sort of musical imitativeness of a bad musical model that was working in me.

Van Doren

Well, now, I remember a poem by Wordsworth called "Resolution and Independence." It begins: "There was a roaring in the wind all night, the rain came heavily and fell in floods." You know, that's a marvelous reconstruction. "But now the sun is rising calm and bright, the birds are singing in the distant woods . . ." You see, the tempest of the night before, and now the peace of the morning, are all in the words. It seemed to me marvelous that a man could do that.

Now, I think the significant thing is that I recognized that something was being done. You know, many people when they read verse, young or old, don't seem to notice anything. They're looking for meaning purely. They're saying, "What is this man saying, and is it true?" Ultimately that is of the greatest importance, but I believe a young person falls in love with reading poetry and with writing it only if it makes some musical sense to him. The Greeks once said, a true poet's lips are touched with honey. There has to be a sweetness in there somehow or other; there has to be a charm in the connection of words with one another.

MacLeish

I agree with you, and that explains in large part the attachment which can be a passionate attachment; but then there's another step involved in the young man—young woman, too—who is determined to go and do likewise, and who is not only determined to, but has to, who's compelled to.

Not all lovers of music want to write music and not all lovers of poetry want to write poetry, but in some cases the nature of the love is such that the only satisfactory use of one's life is to pursue it, and what this is I frankly don't understand.

Van Doren

Well, I think I do; to this extent, at any rate: I think I know in my own case that nothing to me is more pleasing than to have been able to write a

line which I myself like to read over and say to
myself and listen to.

MacLeish

Oh, of course; the greatest delight in the world.

Van Doren

Now, you know the line, "If autumn ended and
the cold light came"? Who wrote that?

MacLeish

Well . . . (laughs)

Van Doren

I was reading you last night, frankly, and I have
been for days. That line at the end of the poem
whose title I forget . . .

MacLeish

"Winter Is Another Season."

Van Doren

"Winter Is Another Season." Well, the whole
thing is wonderful, but suddenly that final line—
it's just like a phrase in music. It signs off.

MacLeish

. . . "Another Country"—which shows what a
good memory I have.

Van Doren

Yes, that's it. "Winter Is Another Country."

25

Well, believe me, I really think that's what it's all about. You know, a fellow who has never written a line that anybody remembers is a woeful person, isn't he? Because poems are made up of lines; we remember some lines and not others.

Down in Washington when Robert Frost had his eighty-eighth birthday celebration—you were not there because you were in Antigua—they asked me to say something, and I said all I was going to do was read the lines of his that I thought anyone would know. And I read two pages of them. After reading them, I remember I said, "That proves the eminence of Robert Frost; the fact that almost everybody knows this many lines of his."

MacLeish

That reminds me of Robert's own phrase, "To write a few little poems it'd be hard to get rid of."

Van Doren

That's right.

MacLeish

But, Mark, to go back to this thing that so fascinates me. I agree with you entirely, it's the mysterious power of words to make music out of meaning, meaning out of music that attracts one to poetry. And it is the hope of being able to accomplish that same end that starts one off. But then there are those long, long, long periods of time in which there is no reason to hope that one can do it.

In my case, for example, I quit the practice of law, as you know, and took a small family to France on next to no means whatever in order to write the poems I wanted to write, at a time when I hadn't written a single line that I thought was any good. Do you remember when you first did something that alarmed you and surprised you into the feeling that by God *you* could do it?

VAN DOREN

Yes, and before that everything I'd written was simply terrible. I got a few things printed in the college literary magazine that I'm ashamed of; I can't bear to look at them. It happened with me all at once several years later. It takes a long time.

But that again is a sign of something important, that you are willing to wait, you're willing to try over and over again. I had a student once bring me some of his poems and I said, "Well, you'll be better ten years from now." But he said, "How can I get through them, those ten years?" (*Mac-Leish laughs.*) And I said: "That's up to you. If you can't get through the next ten years, it's too bad. An artist must be a patient man."

It's a curious thing. I suppose most people think of artists as impatient, but I don't know of any first-rate artist who hasn't manifested in his career an appalling patience, a willingness to wait, and to do his best *now* in the expectation that next year he will do better.

MacLEISH

Yes, Mark, but when you think of the total output in words of most poets, not the enormously prolific ones, but of most poets, and then you think of an entire lifetime spent producing those words, it does indicate that a great deal of time has gone into a very small quantitive product, so that patience and repetitive attack is very much involved. But, Mark, let's go back for a second to this other thing we were talking about.

VAN DOREN

All right.

MacLEISH

It's the "touch of honey on the lips," as you so beautifully put it.

VAN DOREN

I remember saying that that is the thing that finally matters.

MacLEISH

Also, it's the thing that probably matters at the beginning. But at some point also, there's a question of what one has to say. And the importance of what one has to say, with all this music and all this loveliness of pattern, becomes crucial, and that also is a problem that haunts me. The greatest poets have been men who were wise in the sense in which most men are not. Shakespeare certainly *knew* things that nobody else knew.

VAN DOREN

I wouldn't say, Archie, that his distinction was that he knew what nobody else knew. He knew what *everybody* knew.

MACLEISH

He knew what everybody knew, but he *knew* it in a way that nobody else could.

VAN DOREN

That's right. I remember saying once, if I may quote myself, "He was more like everybody else than anybody else was." You know, there are no truly arcane things in him, are there? I mean, those lines of his that stun us, stun us because they are perfect statements of what we already know.

MACLEISH

That's right. Eliot's preferred Shakespearean phrase, "ripeness is all," is something that everybody does know, or should know, but really doesn't quite know until you find that phrase, and that phrase contains it. No matter how one puts this thing, a certain knowledge of what life is, and of what man is, a knowledge of what Keats calls "the hornbook of the heart" of human experience itself, is essential to this enterprise, this strange way of living, this strange undertaking, this writing of poetry.

Van Doren

I think, Archie, you have to want to give your own account of the world. You may not really believe that you see it as nobody else does, but you want to speak of it for yourself, I daresay, in the hope that everyone will understand you even though these things that you say may be of the simplest sort.

I remember a poem of yours which merely talks about the difference between a maple tree and an elm tree, the maple tree rather stiff and holding itself against the wind, and the elm tree letting itself go in streamers. Now at that moment I daresay nothing seemed more important to you than to talk about the difference between a maple and an elm tree. There are those who might say that this was an inconsequential subject. I don't think so, because when I read that poem, all of my experience with those two trees—they're my favorite trees, incidentally—all of my experience was concentrated in a drop of statement.

You know, that poem is only, I suppose, fifty words long. What we all want is to be able to say these things briefly, isn't it? With breathtaking brevity. And many people don't know that poetry is the shortest way of saying things; not the longest, but the shortest.

MacLeish

"Breathtaking brevity" is a wonderful phrase.

Van Doren

But don't you know there are people who think poetry is a roundabout way of speaking? A good poem is the shortest distance between you and the subject. And the subject is something that has struck you very deeply just because it's there, and because it's beautiful and important. Trees are a subject, just as much as a proposition is that you wanted to deliver yourself of, and by the way that's all right too, in poetry. You can write a poem to say a given thing.

You know, people who wonder why anybody likes poetry, or whether poetry is important, people who say that they know nothing about poetry are not telling the truth, because as children they lived with it in Mother Goose, which is a masterpiece of verse. Wouldn't you say?

MacLeish

Yes . . .

Van Doren

You couldn't improve upon it.

MacLeish

Penetrating and unforgettable.

Van Doren

Nobody will ever improve on it. And these same
people who say they know nothing about poetry,
having forgotten Mother Goose, forget also that
they have hymns. Maybe they know ballads; they
know rhymes—"a stitch in time saves nine."
They know popular music. They live with poetry
all the time, and yet they would say that it wasn't
poetry. Whereas it is. It's terribly important to
include everything.

MacLeish

Strangely, *poetry,* as a word, has gotten itself
shoved off into a corner where it applies to something rather specific, rather recondite, rather difficult to grasp. How much is this the fault of
members of the generation of poets to which you
and I belong? It wasn't true of the Victorians,
was it?

Van Doren

No, I think not. I think people read it much more
naturally then.

MacLeish

Tennyson was certainly read voluminously and . . .

Van Doren

. . . think how Byron had been read, and Keats.

People began to read Keats again with great passion and with a sense of commitment and conviction. As a matter of fact, all during this time Shakespeare was being read and seen. You know, a great many people use the word *poet* as if Shakespeare were not an example. Isn't that true? (*Both laugh.*)

MacLeish

Absolutely right.

Van Doren

Many people seem to think the meaning of the word *poet* would exclude Shakespeare. "He's not a poet because he's so interesting."

Archie, you know we're talking about something that often troubles me. In our time I suspect a lot of great things have lost their meaning, and one of them is *poetry*. It is almost as unfortunate a word as the word *art*. I wish the word *art* didn't exist. You know, the Greeks had no such word. They just had the word *teknik*—technique. The *teknik* of doing anything was knowing *how* to do it.

MacLeish

And a poet is a maker.

Van Doren

A maker.

33

MacLeish

And he knows how. And they knew how.

Van Doren

We have more aesthetics these days than we have art. We have theories of art.

MacLeish

I was never so conscious of the effort to remove the word *poet* from the common vocabulary than on the occasion when I was before the Senate Foreign Relations Committee for confirmation as an Assistant Secretary of State. The word *poet* was pronounced with a particular intonation by a certain Senator from Missouri—and I don't mean Mr. Truman. The implication of the intonation being that this man regards himself as a poet and this obviously disqualifies him not only for public life, but for those sensible conversations, the discourse of common sense, by which ordinary men communicate.

Van Doren

I don't know whether you ever read something that Herbert Agar wrote about that very thing. He said, I think, "What a society we would have if that Senator had meant, not that you were a poet, and therefore should not be appointed, but that you should not be appointed because you were a bad poet." See?

34

MacLeish

Yes.

Van Doren

The implication would be that the Senator had read many poets and had a knowledge of them, and had judgments about them, and so . . .

MacLeish

I'm not sure this wasn't a little on his mind.

Van Doren

No, no, no, I'm sure it wasn't at all. That's the whole point. You see, what I mean is this: it's almost staggering to try to conceive of a society in which United States Senators would argue over the relative merits of men in terms of their poetry. The Senator wasn't judging your *poetry* at all.

MacLeish

Yes, I see what you mean. This touches another matter, Mark, and that is the relation of the art of poetry, the relation of being a poet, to the public life. What I have in mind, of course, is that long, long, long decade of the thirties in which some poets began using poetry in a specifically propagandist way with regard to public questions.

Van Doren

Questions of public order?

35

MacLeish

Yes, public order.

Van Doren

Or public disorder.

MacLeish

And yet something, Mark, something was certainly wrong in the activities of the thirties. Something was wrong in the so-called social consciousness of some poems of that period. I'd like nothing better than to try to explore that and to find out what it was that was wrong.

I feel this way about myself. I think some of my poems which moved into this field and were filled with political passion either berating the Marxists or berating their opposites, and so forth, were trespassing; not trespassing exactly, but they had gone over the fence. Something, something went wrong there.

Van Doren

Well now, I remember a poem of yours at a later time. It was about Larry Duggan. The first line was, I think, "God help that country where informers thrive."

MacLeish

Yes.

36

VAN DOREN

And your poem appeared in a newspaper. I believe it was the *New York Herald Tribune*. You were very indignant, obviously. As I read that poem that day, in that morning's paper, I realized that you were simply blazing.

MACLEISH

Right!

VAN DOREN

Now, don't you think that's a right thing to do? Don't you think there were many people who understood you?

MACLEISH

I think the wrath was right. And I think that wrath might perhaps provide a touchstone for a poem attempting to involve itself in a political situation in an effective way. On the other hand poems which got involved with criticisms of the techniques of Marxism, criticisms of the social order, and so forth and so on, these somehow or other went wrong.

VAN DOREN

Well, that might be because the thought itself was shallow. Now, Archie, I'm not referring to your poem. I'm referring to a whole body of poetry.

37

MacLeish

I know.

Van Doren

What I mean by shallow is *new and not truly lived with*. I don't think anyone should write a poem about a subject that has just recently interested him. Now in the case of Duggan, of course, there was the wrath of that particular moment in your own mind, but behind it, over the years, there had been building up—had there not—a very powerful feeling about that sort of thing?

MacLeish

Yes, about the whole McCarthy episode. Yes.

Van Doren

Yes, and this was just the last example for you. So it was not a new subject for you. But you know, time is a terribly important thing. Remember we talked about patience some time ago. Time must pass. You must live with an idea, you must live with a feeling, live with a set of ideas and make them thoroughly yours. I'm not referring to you, because I've read your poems and public statements, and you know I've always read them with the greatest affection.

MacLeish

I know what you mean.

38

VAN DOREN

With most writers it didn't work that way. They just talked, and by the next day they were saying something different. Well, that invalidates what you say today.

MACLEISH

It does. Yes. It invalidates what you say today.

VAN DOREN

Look at that, Archie. Look at that nest. What sort of bird's nest would you say it is?

They stop, and examine the nest.

MACLEISH

I don't know. It could be an oriole's. You know, Ardrey, a playwright who wrote *African Genesis,* has a study of a new theory of what we come out of. He has an account of a bird which makes a very peculiar nest, a nest with a peculiar kind of horsehair knot which only this bird builds. The eggs of the bird were taken from the nest, put under canaries—because they're little tiny birds —and hatched. That generation, when it laid eggs, was again subjected to the canary detour. And, I think, at the end of three generations the birds were released and allowed to go their way, and they built exactly the same peculiar nest without any parental direction whatever.

39

VAN DOREN

It's amazing. They didn't know, because they'd never seen such a nest.

MACLEISH

Somewhere in their genes there's that knot of horsehair.

VAN DOREN

Well, I remember a friend of mine in Cornwall who one evening heard a certain bird, and said, "That's such and such kind of bird." I've forgotten what it was. And he said, "Let's go and look at its nest." I said, "Is it a specially interesting nest?" He said, "Yes, there'll be a little bit of snakeskin hanging from it." We went, and sure enough there was a little bit. You know, it was the snakeskin that's sloughed. Nobody knows why that bird does it, but he does it. Now, isn't that incredible? There it was, perfectly visible, rather raggedly stuck in and hanging down like a flag of danger, or warning, or heaven knows what.

MACLEISH

Maybe the bird feels it keeps off the evil eye.

MacLeish and Van Doren move off again, down the slope.

VAN DOREN

Well, Archie, you were talking about the role of

the poet in society. I suppose in the long run it doesn't make any difference what you thought it was, or what anyone else thinks it was, the final thing that matters is whether or not he wrote a few or many poems that cannot be got rid of. You know, in a given generation the role of the poet can be thought to be this or that, but after generations and even centuries pass it doesn't matter. The question is whether or not, after so much time has passed, people then can read some of a man's poems and be charmed by them. That's what ultimately matters.

MacLeish

I don't know what your feelings are about Shelley but . . .

Van Doren

I don't like Shelley.

MacLeish

I don't either. And yet I have the greatest admiration in the world, the greatest admiration for his courage, his directness, his passion. Nevertheless his poems become increasingly difficult to read.

Van Doren

Well, except in a few cases, a few short poems. You remember, "Music, when soft voices die, vibrates in the memory."

MacLeish

Yes.

Van Doren

You wonder how he was able to write that. I
was reading a lot of Shelley a year or so ago, just
because I have been dismissing him and I thought
it was only fair to read him again. I'm sure any
poet would like to be read. That's all he wants.
So I read him, and I found that he really boiled
down to some very, very perfect short things.
His long poems, his political poems and whatnot
I couldn't read, even though I think his ideas were
right.

MacLeish

Yes, so do I.

Van Doren

But that doesn't matter.

MacLeish

This is a mysterious thing. One thinks Shelley's
ideas were right; that this is exactly the position an idealistic man, a man of reason, of hu-
manity, a man of power and force ought to take.
And yet somehow they drag, whereas Keats becomes fuller and rounder and larger to me every
time I go back to him.

Van Doren

Yes, me too. And in his case, as he himself made

abundantly clear in his letters, it wasn't ever an *idea* that exercised him. Well, then, what was it?

MacLeish

It wasn't an idea that exercised him. There was a passionate belief in life, and belief in love of the human possibility. The end of the "Ode to a Nightingale," which returns the listeners to his *sole* self, is certainly not a return of defeat. It's a return of the realization of the immediacy and reality of actual human life on this earth as distinguished from that escape which can lead anywhere. To me, this central feeling of Keats is more and more—if you'll forgive the word—his manhood, his passion for man, and his participation in that passion.

Van Doren

Yes, and the world that he likes so much, and loves so much, and values so highly was here and now. You see, the thing that bores me about Shelley is that his reference is always to some future, as if this world weren't something in itself. I've often wondered what Shakespeare would have thought, what the expression on his face would have been, if you'd said, "Mr. Shakespeare, where do you think the world is going?" (*Both laugh.*) He'd say: "Going? Why I thought it was here. I thought it couldn't move." (*They laugh again.*) He would say: "Why, all one can do is take in what's here. The earth is full of wonder-

43

ful and vile people, lovely and hideous people, and they all belong, everything belongs, it's just here. And things don't change." There is no future for a man like Shakespeare. You see, those who want the world to become unrecognizable are very suspect with me.

MacLeish and Van Doren enter onto a path paralleling a narrow, fast-running stream in deep woods. They go along quietly for a way, and then:

VAN DOREN

That's a beautiful birch.

MACLEISH

Yes, that's the paper birch. That's the kind of birch that was food, clothing, stationery, shelter, and navigation for Indians.

VAN DOREN

How could they use it for clothing?

MACLEISH

They used it as a sort of vest, a jacket. And of course they wrote on it, and they made canoes out of it. And there was a certain property in the bark that had excellent vitamins or something, and they knew that. Do you have the real paper birch down in Cornwall?

VAN DOREN

Yes, we have all kinds, as I see you have here. There's the black birch and the yellow birch.

MACLEISH

Yellow birch is the heaviest of all, I think. That's what they made ox yokes of. They had a pattern, an ox-yoke pattern. They're always cut a certain way, and they laid that on a log and trimmed it to size.

VAN DOREN

Would you call that a yellow birch? That's what I call yellow birch.

MACLEISH

No, I wouldn't. I'd call that a paper birch too.

MacLeish and Van Doren again walk the woods path for a while in silence; only the sound of walking over last year's fallen leaves can be heard. The air is rich with the dust of the crushed leaves. They cross a stream and move up a slope to a grassy level which reaches to a small dammed trout pond, the lower pond, located behind and below the Uphill Farm main house. They rest in weathered wooden deck chairs.

VAN DOREN

Archie, do you remember when you drove down to see us in Cornwall and there was a smell of

45

smoke in the air? It was in the autumn and there was a forest fire, a big one. And that related itself for you to other things; the visit, and also the state of the world at that moment. I wouldn't say that you were breaking absolutely new ground there, but wouldn't you say the image was potent because you had written many poems back over many years about the burning that was to follow, of smoke in the autumn?

MacLeish

Wonderful evocative power that has. Have you any idea why? An association with childhood perhaps? A very pungent fragrance in childhood? And yet people born in cities who've never really smelled burning leaves also respond to the smell of burning leaves. There's an aspect of that odor that is in some way related to us, to psychological experiences.

Van Doren

Speaking of which, do you notice a strong fragrance of skunk that lies here?

MacLeish

Yes.

Van Doren

What does that do to you? Do you find it attractive?

46

MACLEISH

I rather like it.

VAN DOREN

So do I.

MACLEISH

I like strong smells.

VAN DOREN

I gather, Archie, that on the whole fall is the best season for you, isn't it?

MACLEISH

For you too?

VAN DOREN

Yes, it is. For instance, when I decided to half retire from Columbia, and live in Cornwall the other half of each academic year, I elected to live up there in the fall.

MACLEISH

I remember you did.

VAN DOREN

Some people said, "Why didn't you take the spring?" But no, I love the fall. I love it because of the smells that you speak of; and also because things are dying, things that you don't have to take care of any more, and the grass stops growing.

47

MACLEISH

The human situation improves as the dominance
of vegetation falls away. But this is true more in
New England than elsewhere, don't you think?

VAN DOREN

Probably.

MACLEISH

Do you know Illinois well enough to know how
you feel about the autumn in Illinois?

VAN DOREN

Yes, I do, but it was first powerful for me here, I
mean in New England. Amazingly beautiful and
sudden. It comes quite suddenly, as all the sea-
sons do. We suddenly know it's spring, we suddenly know it's winter when the first snow falls.

MACLEISH

Do you have New England blood?

VAN DOREN

None whatever.

MACLEISH

My mother was a Yankee from Connecticut,
which might explain my addiction. But almost
everyone feels it. I mean, don't most of your
friends, whether they have New England associations or not, love New England?

48

VAN DOREN

Oh yes, I've always remembered a student, a boy who had never been out of New York City as far as I know, who had been reading Frost. He liked it very much, and I asked, "Why in particular?" And he said, "He makes me homesick for New England." I said, "Have you ever been there?" He said, "No. No, but it's somehow everybody's first home. It's a kind of Paradise."

MACLEISH

It is.

VAN DOREN

It's the Paradise out of which we were put.

MACLEISH

But why is that so—everyone's first home? Historically it is everyone's first home. I mean for those who didn't come in through the Virginia Gates. And yet generations passed through here very rapidly, and the life was hard and difficult. On this little farm here, for example, a family named Arms lived for about 150 years. I have their books, and they never had more than $300 in cash, or the equivalent of cash—something they could sell. And yet they put their children through college. Which means the children from their earliest age had to work. It must have been a very difficult life, a hard life, a cold life. And yet they loved New England, and for the New

49

Englanders who went West it persists through the second, third, fourth, fifth generation.

VAN DOREN

Yes.

MACLEISH

Is this a testimonial to the beauty of the land, the movement of the land?

VAN DOREN

I think so, and to the poverty of the land. Its very poverty somehow recommends it. The stones that pop out and make the fields so hard to till are themselves surpassingly beautiful. You know, the boulders, the ledge that we like to have picnics on. I think it was Thucydides who said that the distinction of Athens rested upon the poverty of its soil. People loved that poor country. They also had to sharpen their wits in order to live on it. And so they became the great traders and the great seagoers, and finally the great philosophers and poets that they were.

MACLEISH

When one goes into western Illinois now, where I was about a month ago, for a very considerable stretch of road, perhaps a hundred miles going out toward Rockford, you go through the richest land possible; it's black, deep earth, with the crops coming out of it almost as if they were forced out of it by the exuberance of the land.

And yet it somehow or other doesn't hold you. It's complete in itself. It doesn't demand anything of you. And this does, the land here. It has demanded so much.

VAN DOREN

I think that's it. You have to put so much into it. And you notice the people who live here only as we do, as in a kind of Paradise, work awfully hard to make our places right. We cut trees to make views, and we landscape.

MACLEISH

And yet the poverty of the land, the poverty of the land is only poverty for certain purposes—for plowing. And yet for other purposes there are the trees, the richness of the green, and the depths of the little pockets of soil.

VAN DOREN

I was born out there in the Midwest, you know, and my father had a farm in a very rich part of Illinois. I remember my brother became a farmer and studied agriculture. I remember once asking him this question: I said, "How deep is the loam here? You know, the black loam?" He said, "It's just like this for sixty feet." But here you can't dig more than eight inches.

MACLEISH

Ada has made a lovely flower garden at home; it was really by the process of pulling the rocks out,

51

putting them into a wall, and then using what was around the rocks, little handfulls of rich wonderful land.

VAN DOREN

I understand the original farmers here first cleared the fields by dragging and rolling the stones off to the edge and leaving them in straggling piles. It was only after another generation that they felt wealthy enough to hire someone, if they didn't do it themselves, to build them into walls. And, of course, they wanted something high enough to keep cattle.

I also think there was a pride; they wanted something good looking like the stone walls of England. You know, in certain parts of England they have those marvelous stone walls, rather high and narrow in some cases.

MACLEISH

On the way to the upper pond there's a whole network of walls which obviously at one time surrounded pastures, orchards, and so forth; an ungrateful land, and yet every little piece of it had to be used.

VAN DOREN

I wonder what the future of New England is? There are those who say that it should all go back to forest virtually, because agriculturally it's not very important. There are those who want to make everything—make all of Connecticut—something like a state forest. I lament this.

MacLeish

But to go back to forests would be to lose the meadows. It's the clearings that count, isn't it?

Van Doren

Yes, the difference between one thing and another. New England is full of difference. You know the thing I think that makes people fascinated by New England as they drive through it in the summertime is that it's always changing; you go on around a corner and there's a new landscape. Every landscape tends to be unique. There are no two pockets of valley, no two ridges of hill, that are the same. And it's small and perfect, too. You see, it isn't grandly sweeping.

MacLeish

It has its grandeur, though, Mark; when you get up into that country of Frost's, up in the White Mountains.

Van Doren

Oh yes.

MacLeish

It opens into reaches of grandeur. Connecticut is a land of man-sized hills. The hills bear the right

53

proportion to human beings, and they don't dominate you, and they don't sneer at you.

VAN DOREN

Well, Connecticut of course is different from every part of New England, as every part is different, and yet I feel at home here. Your place here, Archie, is very much like our world. We have a pond about this size, for instance. This is made from a brook, isn't it, that's dammed?

MACLEISH

Yes. I dammed that brook back in the days when I could still dam things.

VAN DOREN

Did you do it yourself?

MACLEISH

Yes, I did it myself with the aid of a neighbor down the hill, and a pair of white horses.

VAN DOREN

Good.

MACLEISH

Not oxen, white horses. The thing that you described had happened; the man who cleaned that field up there had rolled all the rocks down here. There was a great pile of them. And with the aid of these two white horses we built a dam that starts over here against the ledge and goes all the way to the opposite ledge. And having then completed what is a magnificent engineering work, this brook went right through it as though it weren't there at all. (*Van Doren laughs.*) We then grouted in cement, as old man Bush said. He's my neighbor down the hill.

VAN DOREN

What did that mean, "grouted in"?

MACLEISH

When you grout cement in, you sort of grout it in, you know.

VAN DOREN

No, I still don't know. Push it in, you mean?

MACLEISH

Well, yes. You set your rocks, and then you move the cement down in the interstices, you see.

VAN DOREN

Oh, I see.

MACLEISH

But of course you never get it down all the way.

VAN DOREN

No, no.

MACLEISH

So then we had to build an apron in front of it, of earth. And then we covered the apron with these cement steps. Eventually we got something that holds water, more or less.

VAN DOREN

You know, there's nothing more fun than monkeying with water, trying to make it stay somewhere. It won't stay anywhere, you know. Given enough time that dam would go, wouldn't it?

MACLEISH

Oh, of course.

VAN DOREN

Without your mending it.

MACLEISH

It'll go. And it'll be a nice ruin with streams flowing through the bottom of it, and a hole.

VAN DOREN

I was told once that during the Civil War you knew where a New England regiment had been encamped in Virginia. If it was among the hills, when they left there were little paddle wheels turning.

MACLEISH

Really?

VAN DOREN

> The men in their spare time would go up and up and up the brook. Each one would whittle his little pieces of wood and just for the fun of it start them whirling in the water.

> *A fish breaks through the surface of the lower pond, falls back flatly, and is gone.*

MACLEISH

> See that trout jump?

VAN DOREN

> Yes.

MACLEISH

> You have no interest in seeing me pull a trout out of there? I know you're against pulling trout.

VAN DOREN

> No, I'm not against it. I'm simply not a fisherman. Go ahead and do it. I wish you would. Could you? I dare you. I don't think you can.

MACLEISH

> I doubt if I can, but I can try.

VAN DOREN

> What kind of trout are they?

MACLEISH

> They're rainbow.

VAN DOREN

>Good. Rainbow. We have brook trout in our
>pond. They come down naturally out of the
>brook which is diverted into the pond. And I'm
>just satisfied to watch them. I think the neighbors
>fish them out, because there are never too many
>there.

>*MacLeish goes to a shed set in a stand of trees
>near the pond. He returns with fly-casting tackle
>and a net. He and Van Doren go off together,
>across the apron of the dam, to a sunny open flat
>bordering the pond. MacLeish begins to cast
>under the low-hanging branches of an alder, where
>the trout had jumped. All is quiet except for the
>whipping of the casting line. A trout glides be-
>neath the ripples.*

MACLEISH

>Well, there he is. He's out there. I'm going to
>catch that boy!

VAN DOREN

>There's one. See.

MACLEISH

>That's a bullhead.

VAN DOREN

>Yes, that's not a trout.

MacLeish   (*as he casts for the trout*)
            Come on! Come on! Come on! Come on! The
            trouble is, Mark, you're on the side of the fish.
            You don't want me to catch a fish.

Van Doren
            You're wrong. I don't care.

MacLeish   (*laughing*)
            Oh, dear, that's too bad. I had one interested,
            but he's not interested any longer.

Van Doren
            Well you could throw it out a bit further.

MacLeish
            If I could drop that a little—if it would sink a
            little bit more. Come on, Joe! See, the trouble is,
            that damn thing won't sink. I'll let that go down
            in there.

Frog
            Garumph!

Van Doren
            You know, if you wait for a frog to make a noise,
            he won't make any. He waits until you stop wait-
            ing, and then he does it.

Frog
            Garumph!

59

VAN DOREN *(laughs)*
You don't know how much derision there is in that, do you?

MACLEISH
It's sort of sad.

VAN DOREN
You know, the Latin name for him was Rana. That's a good name for him. Don't you think so?

MACLEISH
Yes.

VAN DOREN
At Cornwall, a frog was sounding off under my study, and I got to thinking about the fact that his decision to speak had nothing to do with my desire to hear him speak. And I wrote a poem about it.

FROG
Garumph!

VAN DOREN
"It is not for me his intervals are, it is not to me he says what he says—ah, there he is." I just remembered the end of that thing.

MACLEISH
Well, this is very mysterious.

60

VAN DOREN

Now you're on there.

MACLEISH

Oh, am I caught?

VAN DOREN

Yes.

MacLeish moves back to a laurel to unsnag his trout fly; he returns.

VAN DOREN

Did you break the line?

MACLEISH

I just broke the leader. I was going to change the fur anyway.

VAN DOREN

And the hook too.

MACLEISH

Yes.

VAN DOREN

Do you know a lot about flies?

MACLEISH

No. And I'm persuaded that nobody else does either.

61

VAN DOREN

Well, there are those who claim they know. And
they have their cans and stuff.

MACLEISH

It's funny, you know, that one trout we saw
came out of there as though he meant business.
I'd like to get him.

*He attaches a new wet fly and continues to cast,
letting the lure sink slowly each time, searching
the water off the far shore of the pond.*

VAN DOREN

Is the shade a good place?

MACLEISH

That's where they lie.

*The line suddenly straightens, and as suddenly
slackens.*

VAN DOREN

There! Oh, it's gone. What did you have? Didn't
you have something?

MACLEISH

That was a bullhead.

VAN DOREN

Oh. Are the bullheads edible?

62

MacLeish

Yes, they're quite good.

Van Doren

But they're not a game fish, obviously. There are some small ones just floating around like little submarines.

MacLeish

Come on now, boy. Provide! Provide!

Van Doren

They aren't going to do anything for us. They don't see what we do for them, so they aren't going to do anything for us.

Suddenly, MacLeish has a strike. He plays the run of the fish.

MacLeish

Come on, boy, come on! Mark, I'm going to need that net pretty soon.

Retrieving some of his line, he surfaces the fish, fifteen inches of rainbow trout.

Look at that!

Van Doren

That's a beauty, Archie.

MACLEISH

Yes, he's one of the standard size.

VAN DOREN

Look at his spots.

*The fish begins his final run; MacLeish plays
him against the spring of the rod.*

MACLEISH

Come on, boy! This would be terrible if I missed
him now.

Van Doren hands him the landing net.

VAN DOREN

You lose him? No, you won't lose him.

MACLEISH

Well, I could. Oh!

*He sweeps the trout up from the water with the
net.*

VAN DOREN

The skillful fisherman nets his fish. There, good
work.

MACLEISH

Not very good work. Terrible work.

64

VAN DOREN

No. He's a handsome fellow. Isn't that funny, at the last minute, you got him. Who told you to come down here, by the way?

MACLEISH

You did.

VAN DOREN *(applauding)*

Archie, I am proud to know you.

MACLEISH

He is tremendous, isn't he?

VAN DOREN

And I always thought of you merely as a fisher of men.

MACLEISH *(laughing)*

Now you know I can't even fish for fish.

VAN DOREN

Well, I saw you do it.

MACLEISH

He's losing his color now, poor boy.

VAN DOREN

Perch lose their color very fast too. You know, when Audubon hunted birds to paint, he'd have

65

to get a bird into his cabin on the ship on the Ohio River within minutes and start painting it, or it would lose its color, its iridescence.

MacLeish

The feathers themselves?

Van Doren

The feathers would change, would lose their color. The oil in them would begin to withdraw. You know, Audubon was whipped by his father at the age of nine because he was drawing birds instead of studying Latin. He knew that early what he wanted to do. This was somewhere in the West Indies, where he lived.

MacLeish

Well, I think if I left this fellow here for a while we could walk up to the upper pond and see if we couldn't spot that wood duck we've seen there. He's absolutely marvelous. Are you game for another hundred yards up to the pond?

Van Doren

Game for anything. Do you get better fishing up there?

MacLeish

No, but it's a lovely pond. And the ducks are there.

He secures the fish on a stringer, and then places his fishing tackle along the length of a fallen tree. MacLeish and Van Doren start along the path leading to the upper pond.

VAN DOREN

Look at this iris. Now, did that just come there?

MACLEISH

No, I planted those.

VAN DOREN

Oh, you did.

MACLEISH

Do you see the Siberian iris there at the end of the dam?

VAN DOREN

Yes.

MACLEISH

That's the same Siberian iris that we saw along the stream down below.

VAN DOREN

Well, it carried down.

MACLEISH

Think so?

67

Van Doren

Oh, surely.

MacLeish

The seed floats down?

Van Doren

Our iris, on our pond, keeps spreading, always downstream.

MacLeish

Well, let's head up to the pond.

They move along the path through the narrow band of woods separating the ponds.

Van Doren

Now will you explain to me why the birch takes life so hard? Why does a birch bend and come way over, whereas other trees will break off? You know, it's amazing how flexible a birch is. Once they are held long enough, they get frozen in that position. Look here, Archie, just with my thumbnail I was able to get some of the birch-bark off. Now smell it. How aromatic it is!

MacLeish

Oh yes. That's wonderful.

Van Doren

Isn't that lovely? There's no other birch that smells like that.

They hesitate at the edge of the woods bordering the earthwork dam containing the upper pond.

Is this the source of the brook on your place, or does it go beyond?

MacLeish

This is the source right here. If we're quiet we may see that wood duck I spoke to you about. When I'm walking through the woods I see him sometimes on the far side of the pond. Maybe he'll show up again. Of course, he's a wild thing, and he may be somewhere else now.

Van Doren

Don't I hear something rustling over in there?

MacLeish

No, I think it's the wind.

They are quiet for a long moment, looking, listening; then they move onto the earthwork dam and stretch out in the dry grass.

Well, he's not here. He must have heard us coming through the woods.

Van Doren

How deep does this pond get?

MacLeish

Six or seven feet. Like to take a swim?

69

VAN DOREN (*laughing*)

You remember, in Antigua we did snorkeling? You didn't tell me, but you were a little bit worried about me. You knew I wasn't a water man. So when I was ready to try snorkeling, there you were, waiting to catch me if I went down or something.

MACLEISH

Well, there are things that happen in the water down there.

VAN DOREN

I know they do. And you're not supposed to skin yourself on the coral because you get an infection. But it was a lovely experience, just the little bit that I did. Archie, how much of the time, now that you're free to spend every year just as you want to, how much of the year do you think you'll spend in Antigua?

MACLEISH

I think probably just what we did before. I'd just like to go down there and spend a little time. That is, I'd like to spend as much time as possible up here. Then I have that hankering for Cambridge, you know.

VAN DOREN

Uh-hum.

MacLeish

Do you go back up to Columbia a good deal?

Van Doren

Not a great deal, no. When I'm in New York I'm usually there on some errand which takes me elsewhere; and when I'm through I'm home.

MacLeish

You know, that's one of the things in your life that fascinates me. You'll forgive my putting it baldly, but certainly, in addition to everything else, you're the great teacher of our generation. And yet when you got to the point when you could, you didn't hesitate a minute to decide that you were going to stop teaching and take all your time to yourself. Wasn't that a real wrench when you did it? Didn't you find that you depended an awful lot on teaching—by the plowing up of students and so forth—for the manuring of your ground?

Van Doren

Well, no. I think I never felt any wrench at all. Maybe there was one, and I should have felt it, but I had done it for forty years, and that's a long time, you know.

MacLeish

Forty years is a long time.

71

VAN DOREN

I don't mean I was tired of it.

MACLEISH

You had never done it over and over and over. You were always breaking new ground, you were always doing new things.

VAN DOREN

It was awfully interesting. I really liked it a great deal.

MACLEISH

Did you like it at the beginning? When you started out as a poet supporting himself by teaching, which is what your situation was, did you resent the teaching or did you like it from the very beginning?

VAN DOREN

I liked it from the very beginning. I had students who interested me a great deal. I remember in my first class, my very first class, I had Whittaker Chambers and Lionel Trilling. (*Laughs*.) Isn't that amazing?

MACLEISH

That is amazing. What sort of memory do you have of Whittaker Chambers?

VAN DOREN

He was a very, very affectionate, warmhearted

boy, who wrote extremely well. He was very intelligent. But during that first term—oh, around November—he began to be remiss with his papers. He wasn't turning in things, and I thought I ought to call him in—he was a freshman—and tell him this, warn him. He said, "Well, I'm so busy with politics that I can't keep up with my work." I said, "Politics? What are you doing?" And he said, "I'm distributing handbills for Calvin Coolidge for Vice-President. I'm trying to get him elected Vice-President." (*MacLeish laughs.*) He was a passionate Republican.

MacLeish

Was he really?

Van Doren

Yes. So much so that he was sacrificing his marks and everything. Within a year or so he was something else.

MacLeish

Was this a process of continual change, back and forth?

Van Doren

He was always changing.

MacLeish

Did you keep in touch with him?

73

VAN DOREN

Oh, yes, yes. He used to come down and see us. And, later on, he would write us. He went off on his own all around the world, and he would write me letters and send me poems. He was a good poet.

MACLEISH

He was?

VAN DOREN

Oh, yes. I used to print some of his poems in *The Nation,* when I was Literary Editor of that. He was a Communist within five years. He was a Coolidgeite in the fall of '20, and in '25 he wrote me a postal card saying, "Today I joined the Communist Party." I don't know about the stages in between.

MACLEISH

Now, if that had been five or ten years later in the history of the world, one would have understood it, but I should have thought 1925 was hardly a period when an intelligent young American would go for Communism.

VAN DOREN

Well, now, I could be wrong, but I think that was it. I think it was that early.

MACLEISH

Mark, what would you say, what *do* you say to

74

youngsters who ask you how in the world they're going to support themselves while they try to turn themselves into poets? Do you tell them you think teaching is a good thing to do? Or do you think it depends wholly on the person, or do you just not answer that question? Because you certainly must get asked it.

VAN DOREN

Yes, I was always asked it. In the first place, they wanted to know whether I thought they could become writers, regardless of how they lived meanwhile.

MACLEISH

Would you answer that question?

VAN DOREN

You know, it's an impossible question. I used to say, "Only God knows." But that didn't tell them very much. So finally, one day when I was talking to such a student, I said, "Oh dear, let's see. Do you like coffee?" And he said, "I'm crazy about coffee." I said: "Well, you have a chance. Because most writers I know love coffee." (*MacLeish laughs.*) Well, he got the point right away. That's all the point I had.

MACLEISH

Oh, you really can't answer that question; at least I don't think you can.

75

VAN DOREN

Of course you can't, because their performance to date means almost nothing, does it? After all, it's a matter of what they *will* do. And after all, nobody knows what anybody will do.

I was talking once with a personnel man who interviewed men for a business house, a big financial house in New York. I said, "How do you do it?" He said, "Well, we have interviews, we have examinations, we have tests, and so forth." I said, "Can you really know whether a man will be good in the long run?" He said: "No, because what we don't know is what he'll be like five years from now. We can measure his intelligence as of this moment, and his ambition; but will he keep his ambition? We don't know."

MACLEISH

Well, so you don't answer the first question, which is: "Am I a writer?" What do you do about the second question, which is: "Here I am, twenty-two years old; if I am a writer, obviously I've got to support myself in some way. Should I be a teacher?" Will you answer that question?

VAN DOREN

I never recommended teaching, unless they wanted to very much. If they wanted to, that was a different thing. I always encouraged them to live on as little as possible while they tried it out. I said, "Borrow money. Take it from your parents." I used to beg them to let their parents support them longer than they felt they ought to. I said, "Your parents will never forgive you if it turns out that you didn't let them help you do something that you couldn't have done for yourself at this point." I said, "Live any old way you want to and just try it." Of course, it's awfully hard, and they usually couldn't stand it. But I didn't specifically recommend teaching or anything else.

MacLeish

Of course, I never taught as a young man, and therefore I have no idea what it is. By the time I took to teaching I was in my late fifties. And I, after all, did start as Boylston Professor, instead of starting as . . .

Van Doren

As an instructor.

MacLeish

. . . as an instructor. I had the feeling, from what I saw of young friends of mine in the graduate school, young friends of mine who were teaching, instructors and assistant professors, that that profession, at least in a big college and at least in your early years, can be a very trying one, a very competitive one, with a good deal of intramural knifing and politicking. Is that a misstatement, or is that the way it works out?

77

VAN DOREN

I never saw it. And when I retired—well, you may remember the evening when you were so good as to come and take part in some of the festivities . . .

MACLEISH

Yes.

VAN DOREN

You were sweet to do that, with Fredric March and Jim Thurber.

MACLEISH

Oh, that was a wonderful thing.

VAN DOREN

Yes, it was. Well, you may remember that I said at the end, thanking everybody, that I wanted to thank Columbia, because it was a community singularly free of malice, envy and malice. I said I had never seen it. I was told later that I was a simpleton, that there is plenty there, as there is everywhere, but that I just hadn't seen it. I don't know what's true.

MACLEISH

I don't think the answer is that you're a simpleton. I think the answer is that even the most malicious "malicer" wouldn't show malice to you. If you don't mind my saying so.

VAN DOREN

Well, they didn't. And this might be partly because I was not competitive. I didn't care. You
see, I always kept writing uppermost. That was
the main thing. Teaching was always, to me, a
secondary thing. I don't mean it was unimportant,
but it was always under the other. You know, it's
very important to do that if you're a young writer
and have to teach to live. It's just a matter of
will, a matter of an understanding with yourself,
to keep one thing higher than the other in your
mind. You save yourself for that.

MACLEISH

You give it preference at those moments in which
you are at your absolute best and can do.

VAN DOREN

And those moments can come any time, in the
middle of the night, you know.

MACLEISH

Yes.

VAN DOREN

Or even on a train, or going to class. You get
home, and if you really want to write something,
you're not tired. You know, you can do anything
you want to do.

MACLEISH

This is miraculous . . .

79

VAN DOREN

You have all the time in the world.

MACLEISH

. . . this sort of iron discipline of preference, you describe. It's miraculous to me. I could never do it. The moments I have found myself in my lifetime, engaged in something else that had to be done, as, for example, teaching or preparing a lecture, or government work of some kind, I've always felt I had to just put the writing away, put it aside, forget about it, and come back to it when I could. Your attack on it is braver and I'm sure much more fruitful. In fact, the proof is in you. And yet I can't imagine a more unanswerable question. I've never been able to tell a youngster what I thought he ought to do if he really, seriously, wanted to write.

The first thing I would do, would be to let myself go this far, to say: "You owe it to yourself and your friends and your future, to make up your mind whether there is something you want to write or whether you just want to *be* a writer. If that's all you want, go and sell drugs, or do anything, but don't pursue this dream, because *being* a writer is one of the worst things in the world. But if there is something you have to write, then work it out however you can."

Think, Mark, of all the people that you've known and their various ways of resolving it—Joyce, running around Europe from spot to spot and teaching and tutoring in the most unrewarding way, living in the damnedest places. And yet, to use your phrase, keeping the first thing first at all points, and never yielding. Of all the various ways of getting around the problem, there is no real way.

Van Doren

No. No, there's no royal road.

MacLeish

But they're all going into teaching now. All these kids go into teaching.

Van Doren

Yes.

MacLeish

Maybe it'll work, maybe it won't.

Van Doren

Well, you know, teaching itself doesn't need to be a drag on you. There again, it all depends on how you look at it. Teaching shouldn't be something that you do against the grain. I think you should like to teach. You should like to tell people things. You should like to share with students the excitement of reading a certain book, and have a very practical view of that book, a professional view of it.

81

I always tried to be professional, to talk about a book, not as if it were a piece of English literature, you know, or an item in a survey course—never that—but a *book*. Why, I didn't even talk about the author very much. I didn't talk about the history of the times, or anything of the sort. I just wanted them to read well; because, after all, a writer is first of all a reader.

MacLeish

And then, for a nonscholar like myself . . .

Van Doren

I'm not a scholar, by the way.

MacLeish

Well, you went to graduate school.

Van Doren

Yes, yes.

MacLeish

I went through law school which, as all Ph.D's know, is an inferior kind of graduate education.

Van Doren

Oh, I wouldn't say so.

MacLeish

At the same time, I found teaching the best way of learning that I know anything about. You really have to find out what it is you think in order to teach, don't you?

VAN DOREN

Of course you do.

MACLEISH

Well, shall we slide down, Mark, and go back to our hill town, leave this beautiful water?

VAN DOREN

You mean, go back up to the house?

MACLEISH

Back up to the house.

VAN DOREN

You know, this is nice. Look there, Archie. A fish jumped.

MACLEISH

Yes.

VAN DOREN

There are fish up here, too.

MACLEISH

I've seen a couple jump. I think there probably are brook trout left, in spite of the fact I thought they'd all been fished out.

83

They return along the woods path leading down to the lower pond.

VAN DOREN

My, this is fine. I love the patchwork here.

MACLEISH

I do too.

VAN DOREN

With the sunlight coming down.

MACLEISH

A lovely kind of light.

VAN DOREN

You know, the other day I was in our pinewoods. I was cutting some poles for the garden. I looked off at a distance, and it looked as if a pine tree were bleeding. There was a patch of brilliant red on it.

MACLEISH

What was it?

VAN DOREN

A scarlet tanager. The most startling thing was the incredible color. Do you have them here?

MACLEISH

Yes, rarely.

84

VAN DOREN

Yes, they're rare with us. I took Dorothy up the next day to see it. (*Laughs.*) Of course, it wasn't there.

MACLEISH

This is the scene, right here, right in these woods, of the last shooting I ever saw, the last shooting I ever saw Hemingway do. We were coming this way, walking like this in the fall of the year; and two grouse came up out of there, crossed in the clearing here. He got one there, and wheeled and got another right there. It was autumn then, and there were few leaves, so that you could see them against the sky. They both dropped, the first one . . .

VAN DOREN

You mean, he got both of them.

MACLEISH

He got both of them. The first one dropped in here, the second one dropped right on the pond.

VAN DOREN

Wonderful.

MACLEISH

Was he proud!

VAN DOREN

What kind of a gun did he have?

MACLEISH

I think he was using a sixteen-gauge.

VAN DOREN

When was that about, Archie?

MACLEISH

Nineteen thirty.

VAN DOREN

I never knew Hemingway. You knew him in Paris, of course, didn't you?

MACLEISH

I knew him very, very well in Paris. I met him in '24, and over the next four or five years I knew him extremely well. Part of that time after he and Hadley were divorced, before he married Pauline, he lived with us. And then when we came back here, he was up here a good deal. And when I went down to Key West, we were together a good deal. But the inevitable thing happened. The same thing that happened with all his friends, a terrific quarrel about '33 or '34, I think.

VAN DOREN

You say "the inevitable thing." Did Hemingway quarrel with everyone?

MacLeish

Yes, he quarreled with everyone, as he himself knew very well.

Van Doren

In your case was it something you'd rather not talk about?

MacLeish

I wouldn't mind talking about it, but you'd be bored. It was a childish business. It was simply that we'd been together too long out in the Gulf Stream, fishing, and anything we said to each other infuriated us. It was a simple conflict of overexposure.

But you know, Mark, he was a wonderful, an irreplaceable but an impossible friend: a man you couldn't get along with, a man you couldn't get along without.

Van Doren

He was like that?

MacLeish

Yes, that's the way he was. Come on, Mark, let's go home.

MacLeish and Van Doren silently climb the steep pine-studded slope to the main house. Following a long lunch, they relax in the large cool chamber MacLeish uses for a music room and study.

87

MacLeish

One thing we started to talk about this morning was the relation of poetry to the whole political experience. There is another aspect of that; not the validity of a particular poem in seizing on the experience, but—and maybe this was what was wrong with so many poems in the thirties— the attempt of poems at that point, certain poems, to produce consequences, to persuade.

I know a little how you feel about this. We both share the feel of Keats' remark, for example, that we hate poems that have a palpable design upon us. That isn't the word. Or is it? I forget. The real question, though, is: What are the limits of the power of poetry to make things happen in the world? Any? Any limits or any power?

Van Doren

I don't think you should expect poetry to make things happen in the world if you mean by things, actions of individuals or actions of nations. I don't know that poetry has ever had that effect. To the extent that it is real I shouldn't think it ever did anything more than remind us of what the world already is. The world is whatever it is. Now, that is begging a great question, I know, but the world is what it is. And I think—I'd be subject to correction here—I think the function of poetry is to remind us of our own knowledge of what the world is. Because we know what it is already.

88

MacLeish

I think you and I agree on the fundamental position here. I'm sure we do from what you've written and what we've said to each other. I think both of us feel that the real effect of a great poem is to make one really know what he thought he knew. What a great poet does is to bring to knowledge what had become so well known that it ceased to be knowledge at all.

Van Doren

Yes, or it could be that he didn't even think he knew it; he had never been in that part of the world at all with his mind, I mean consciously.

MacLeish

This still raises a question where maybe we do disagree a little. Granted that poetry is, as I would put it, that poetry is an instrument of knowledge in the sense that it brings you to know what otherwise you might not know, or what you might not know vividly, that, in Wordsworth's phrase, it "carries truth alive into the heart with passion," which is a kind of knowing—granted that, doesn't it follow that poetry *does* make things happen—that it is one of the ways things are brought to happen in the world, to bring a living generation to a knowledge of its situation, a knowledge of its dangers, a knowledge of its hopes, of its aspirations, a knowledge of what the world really is in all its potentialities?

In a time—well, let me step back for a minute and quote from a review in the *New York Times Book Review* a while ago which referred to the illness of our time as "a kind of pervading grayness which prevented people from knowing what the meaning of life was." I'm quoting the review. The phrase "meaning of life" comes out of the review, not out of me.

Now, if this is at all true, if it is true that one of the things that happens in our time, one of the things that is wrong, is a sort of grayness, a graying out of an acute sense of what the world is, and what the choices are, and what the possibilities are, isn't it conceivable that the poem, if there were such a poem—and I think you and I would agree that there have been such poems—might make things happen in the sense of bringing a generation to an aliveness of knowledge of where it was and what it was doing?

VAN DOREN

Well, I suppose Eliot's *Waste Land* in 1922 . . .

MACLEISH

That is what I was thinking of.

VAN DOREN

If it did nothing else, it spoke for a generation that had already, by the way, begun to think such things.

MacLeish

Yes, exactly, it had already begun.

Van Doren

Henry Adams' *Education,* which was brought
out for the public in 1918, only four years before, had in a way already done it. I've always
thought that that was a seedbed for *The Waste
Land.* Whether or not that's the case, the almost
immediate response to *The Waste Land,* it seems
to me, proved that a great many people were
thinking that sort of thing and trying to say it.
Eliot said it for them. Was that what you had in
mind?

MacLeish

Yes, that sort of thing. Yeats' "Second Coming," with the definition of a total human situation with which that poem begins, inevitably
produces, I should think, a realization of what
the situation actually is.

What I'm getting at is this. One of our con-
temporaries has said on several occasions that
poetry never makes anything happen. This always strikes me as being not an infuriating remark, but a rather stupid remark, because I
should say that the absolute contrary was true, that
poetry is really one of the few things, if not the
only thing in the world, that *ever* makes anything happen. A new invention doesn't make

anything happen; a war, very few wars change
anything. A lot of people die, there is a lot of
misery and bloodshed, but nothing happens. But
a great poem, a great work of art, a great poem
can make things happen.

VAN DOREN

Well, now in the case of *The Waste Land* what
happened? I would say no more than that people
learned what they already knew.

MACLEISH

But to learn . . .

VAN DOREN

They said, "Yes." They said, "Yes, that's the
kind of world we live in."

MACLEISH

But you *come* to know what you already know,
to know it alive in the heart instead of knowing
it up here dead in the head. It's the difference between reverie and action. And though *The Waste
Land* was not a poem that would produce action,
since it was in effect saying that we live in a
civilizational wasteland, it nevertheless produced
something rather like the wall at the end of a
pool against which the swimmer kicks before he
heads off in the opposite direction. The revulsion
against *The Waste Land* followed very rapidly,
not against *The Waste Land* but against that
world.

Van Doren

Yes. Are you suggesting that "action" might mean in this case "reaction" to the revelation that *The Waste Land* brought? Is that right?

MacLeish

I think so.

Van Doren

So that people, being swimmers in the sea of our life, kicked off from the end of the pool and went into new waters just because Eliot had built a place for their feet to take off from. Is that it?

MacLeish

Or taking it the other way around . . .

Van Doren

The figure is getting a little top-heavy, I'm afraid.

MacLeish

It's a little top-heavy. Another way around is to take a poet whom you and I both admire very much. It seems to me that no one can really read, comprehend, absorb, understand, and make part of themselves Keats' great odes without finding himself in a world in which the value of the human possibility, the value of the human aspiration—the sort of human aspiration that is involved in the couplet at the end of "Ode on a Grecian Urn"—becomes a positive force in his life, much in the same way that it is in Wordsworth. The comprehensions—the conception of man that lies in those poems of Wordsworth that you were saying earlier formed your youth—that conception is a conception which does make things happen.

VAN DOREN

Yes, *happening* in that sense I'm quite willing to accept. I know that you didn't mean that you'd go out suddenly and do something.

MACLEISH

Go out and persuade somebody with one of those pseudo-Fascist "Marching Songs" that Yeats wrote at the end of his life. They certainly made nothing happen on anybody's part except laughter.

VAN DOREN

Now, of course there is a poem that I suppose made a lot of people do lots of things, "The Marseillaise." Undoubtedly it had a lot of effect, didn't it? I can't believe it didn't.

MACLEISH

Well, "The Marseillaise" makes a wonderful bridge. (*Van Doren laughs.*)

VAN DOREN

You see, this is only a reminder of what a broad thing poetry is. It covers not only highly sophisticated works such as Eliot's and Yeats', but songs, for the most part, that nobody knows the author of.

MacLeish

A reminder of what an infinitely suggestible thing a human creature is who can react to this.

Well, this comes to a sort of stage two in this interrogatory of mine. Which is—how shall I put it—what is the effectiveness of a great political statement when it achieves in its metaphor, its imagery, its rhythm, the quality of poetry?

Take, for example, something we've been talking about very recently, Lincoln's message on the State of the Union, December of '62, "My fellow-citizens, none of us can escape history." And that great definition of the American situation, "the last, best hope of earth." Those words in this context, words maneuvered like this, do make things happen. Doesn't rhetoric, then, only make things happen when it has the quality of poetry?

Van Doren

I might point out to you, Archie, that that speech was a failure. You see, he was asking Congress to do something which it refused to do. However, those are wonderful words, I agree; I don't know any better poem than the last paragraph of that speech. Lincoln was a very good poet who wrote in prose, but that speech did not produce the action that Lincoln wanted it to produce. But in you and me, now almost a hundred years . . .

MacLeish

A hundred years this December.

Van Doren

That's right. In you and me now, and many other persons, and in persons all through this past century, it has made a lot of difference. By the way, I'm agreeing in principle.

But you know, Archie, I've never been able to make sure that I knew the distinction between rhetoric and poetry. I don't know if Shakespeare is a great poet or a great rhetorician. What difference does it make? He probably thought of himself as a great rhetorician. I'm sure he was a very crafty and conscious writer. He must have been when you consider what he did, in the time that he did it in; when you consider that he wrote all the speeches of these plays, each of the persons bleeding to death out of his own heart and yet Shakespeare is none of those persons himself. He was merely writing their speeches, quite possibly in cold blood—very, very cold blood—with a coldness of heart which I think only the greatest artists have.

MacLeish

> Yes, Mark, but consider the words, the construc-
> tion of almost all of that last paragraph of Lin-
> coln's message. First of all there is a very strong
> rhythmic form, a form which can practically be
> put into lines if you drop a few sentences out. To
> call the form "Biblical" I don't think really de-
> scribes it; it was his own.

Van Doren

> Yes. Nobody else ever wrote that way.

MacLeish

> Secondly, the language is sensuous and figura-
> tive. And thirdly, the power of it lies in that
> kind of emotional logic with which poetry over-
> whelms you. "Fellow-citizens, we cannot escape
> history. We of this Congress and this adminis-
> tration will be remembered in spite of ourselves."
> Jesus, what a thing to say to a Joint Meeting of
> the Congress! What a wonderful thing to say!
> "No personal significance or insignificance can
> spare one or another of us. The fiery trial through
> which we pass will light us down, in honor or
> dishonor, to the latest generation. . . . We—
> even we here—hold the power and bear the re-
> sponsibility. . . . We shall nobly save or meanly
> lose the last, best hope for us." Well, if that's
> rhetoric let's all be rhetoricians.

Van Doren

> Yes.

MacLeish

Well then, Mark, where do you draw a line between the purely rhetorical and poetry? Do you
have to draw a line? Is it necessary in order to talk
sensibly and effectively about the art of poetry,
to put fences around it? And how do you dis-
tinguish between the poet who makes something
happen, who changes his time in the sense that
we're talking about, and the politician of Lincoln's dimensions who makes a speech which, as
you have pointed out, fails on its occasion, but
lives on to dominate the minds of his country-
men? And does poetry become then, does it include, whatever it is that moves men in their
spirits to an active and positive knowledge of
what it is that they haven't quite known or
haven't known, or haven't known that they knew?
It's a difficult thing to talk about.

Van Doren

Yes, but it's a most important thing to talk about.

MacLeish

I think it's important to talk about.

Van Doren

I think you hit it off extremely well when you
spoke of our knowing freshly and vividly and
deeply what we already knew. Socrates once said
that nobody could learn anything or did learn
anything except what he already knew, but he
didn't know he knew it. A teacher must under-

stand, if he is a teacher, that his students potentially know everything, no matter how young they are. You know, a student who is only seventeen, has lived, after all, on earth seventeen years, and that's a good deal of time. He's been born and he's had parents, he's lived in houses, he's had friends, he's had sweethearts, he's been angry, he's been jealous, he's been proud, he's been ambitious, he's been ashamed. There isn't any passion that he hasn't experienced in one sense or another. Wouldn't you think so?

MacLeish

Yes, I would.

Van Doren

So what folly it is to address a group of freshmen, say in college, as if they were blanks. They're not blanks. They're already filled up. It's necessary to remember how much they know, and to have faith in the knowledge that they do have, and then to assume that they can use their knowledge in understanding Shakespeare or Homer or Walt Whitman or Lincoln.

To be a true teacher, it seems to me, you must assist them to do this very thing that you spoke of, namely, realize what is in them, because that's the only thing that matters. You see, a poem is for the reader finally, isn't it? Surely, it is true for the reader and isn't true for anybody else.

MacLeish

It doesn't exist anywhere else except in the mind of the man who reads it at the moment he reads it.

Van Doren

Exactly.

MacLeish

Otherwise it's a document on a page.

Van Doren

It's pitiful, I think, when poets write—I don't think they really do this, but they sometimes say they write for themselves or for their friends or for other poets. It's pitiful to have them talk that way. They really write for people, unknown people, strangers. An artist is a man writing for strangers, persons he will never know, but nevertheless persons whom he has faith in as being, after all, like himself.

MacLeish

I think the important thing is to make the distinction you are making now and that you have made in your teaching. Between these two kinds of knowing—I know, but I don't really know—the difference is really enormous.

A man knows death. He knows, in other words, that we all die. But he doesn't *know* death. He doesn't *know* what death is until the poignancy of death is driven into his heart as deeply as death itself goes. The only way that any of us have ever known about death, short of dying oneself or having what one most loves in the world die, is through those profound perceptions of art which drive the nail in so deeply you can't shake it loose.

So there are really two kinds of knowing. There ought to be different words for them. One is *knowing*, and the other is *awareness*. Or one is knowing and the other is something else that is keen and sharp and active. And the deepest conviction I have about poetry is that poetry is the only means by which, short of the experience itself, one possesses the experience. Don't you think that is true?

VAN DOREN

Yes. Or you can make this distinction, which might sound semantic; better than knowing *about* something is *knowing* it. You know, we're asked these days to know a lot *about* a lot of things, but to *know* them is a very different thing. Would you accept that as a usable distinction?

MACLEISH

I would, I would.

VAN DOREN

Well, then I think we understand each other very well. I think poetry makes an immense difference in the world, if only that it makes everybody who reads it better; better in the sense of being deeper and more delicate, and more generous in his understanding of what things are, or what himself is. You see, the people in 1862 who read that wonderful paragraph from Lincoln were not used to getting that sort of thing from politicians. You know what they usually got.

MacLeish

They got Buchanan.

Van Doren

Yes, and it never moved them at all. As John J. Chapman said, most of it sounded like "a woodchuck eating a carrot." But here suddenly was a voice speaking, a man speaking. You had no doubt. You see, there is another thing to be considered in the case of this great paragraph. Not only is there rhythm and seriousness, but a *man* seems to be saying it, as if it meant everything in the world to him. He has an almost unspeakable anxiety not to be misunderstood.

MacLeish

This produces a comment on something else that we've been talking about. We began talking about the sort of thing that drives a youngster, with a force beyond his control, into the almost hopeless attempt to master this art of poetry. He's a youngster. He hasn't written anything. He isn't sure he will, but he has to do this; he has to pursue it. And the reason may very well lie in this: that poetry has such an enormous importance in the realization of the experience of life that all the substitutes sort of fall away, and among the substitutes I would put a very large part of fiction, as I'm sure you would.

Far and away the greater part of the fiction that is produced in our time, and far and away the greater part of the drama that is produced in our time, is produced for the purpose, not of bringing one to a complete realization of experience, but in some way or other, by some means or another, the experience is pushed away so that you don't have to think about it. Go to the theater for a lovely escape. Laugh all night. Have a daisy time. Read a novel to find out what it feels like to have somebody else love somebody else, you know.

VAN DOREN

Well, I remember hearing you speak in an interview about *JB* the morning after it opened in New York. You remember there was a strike in the newspapers . . .

MACLEISH

I do indeed. I will never forget that.

VAN DOREN

. . . so that people couldn't read reviews. That was a dreadful blow, I should think, except that you sustained it and the play sustained it. There you were being interviewed, I believe, by Dave Garroway on the program "Today," and I happened to be listening, and you told Dave Garroway about your impulse to write that play.

As I remember it, you said: "In our day immeasurable suffering has been inflicted upon innumerable persons because we live in a very terrible time. Not only have millions and millions of persons died by violence, but millions of persons have been displaced, torn out of their houses and homes and sent somewhere else. It's a world which is almost immeasurable in the amount of suffering that it has endured." And you, thinking about this and wondering how it could be talked about really seriously, not just in terms of statistics, not just in terms of so many millions of this or that, but in terms of its essence, hit upon the figure of Job, who is the very symbol of suffering, undeserved suffering, suffering which nobody can understand.

This seemed to be right to you because you thought most of the people who suffered in the twentieth century did not deserve to suffer. They didn't bring it on themselves. They were victims. Well, is that what you're talking about?

MacLeish

You stated it perfectly, and I'm amazed and astonished that you should remember it so well.

You stated perfectly exactly what I said to Garro-way. And this is exactly what I felt. Just after the Battle of Britain, I went down to West Ham, down the Thames River, below London, east of London, and the thing that was so overwhelming was not the thousands of destroyed houses, the thing that was overwhelming was the people, most of them Scots people.

VAN DOREN

You would find *them* of course.

MACLEISH

Yes, and all of them bewildered and entirely in-nocent victims of Nazi bombing. They got bombed because the curve of the river there made a mark that the bombers could see on a moon-light night as they came over. That was their sin; they lived in a place where the moon shone on the river. And that, and the fact that you found family after family which, bombed out here, had gone to the west of London and had been bombed out there. One family had gone way up into the north of the country and by chance had been bombed out there. There were two of them left out of eight.

Well, this sort of thing makes a sort of pattern of meaninglessness, and to deal with meaninglessness, to deal with tragic meaninglessness, meant to find a metaphor and here was the metaphor, the Book of Job. Now, I won't say—I certainly wouldn't dream of saying—that my play even began to do this. But this is the sort of thing that . . .

VAN DOREN

But it did do it.

MACLEISH

. . . this is the sort of thing that poetry does attempt to do, does it not? Knowledge here begins to be meaning, doesn't it?

VAN DOREN

Well, now take a play that I wrote not too long after you wrote that play; my play about Lincoln, whom, incidentally, we've been talking about here. . . .

MACLEISH

Yes. I was working on *JB* at the same time.

VAN DOREN

Oh, I see. Well, I think I wrote my play about Lincoln simply because, having read for years of Lincoln and around him, read his own works and works about him, having become utterly enthralled by this person, I just had to do something about it. I had to get him talking, I had to put him into action. I wanted to show him to other people as I thought I understood him. I don't claim that I do understand him better than anybody else. But there's no other purpose that that play has in my own mind than to present this very, very great man, this infinitely deep and subtle man.

MacLeish

You seized those last few days of Lincoln's life with extraordinary courage and with poignant focusing of concern. The whole thing, the whole drama, is played out and yet the whole drama is still to be played out. And in a certain sense your play suggests that the soul of America will be saved if we ever come to understand Lincoln's tragedy and triumph.

Van Doren

Yes. If we remember *that* man.

MacLeish

Yes, if we remember *that* man, remember him in terms of understanding.

Van Doren

Of course.

MacLeish

This is the thing that I don't think you can come back to often enough; the tremendous importance of art to make one realize in the gravel of one's gizzard what otherwise might become simply an abstraction in the head.

107

This skirts around another question which uses the same words but in a different way. I think we've been talking about the power of the art of poetry to bring human experience—this chaotic, involved, formless, meaningless, flow-past of life —into focus, giving it shape and giving it significance. Well, now, there's another problem that uses these same words but is quite different, and this is the problem of the relation of a given poet to the experience of his time. For example, you have Keats dying at twenty-six, I think it was; writing the great odes at twenty-five; writing the sonnet about Chapman's Homer at, what, seventeen or eighteen?

VAN DOREN

Something like that, yes.

MACLEISH

What experience had he had but the experience of an apothecary shop and the experience that came to him through art?

VAN DOREN

And through reading Shakespeare and Spenser and Milton.

MACLEISH

And there was Blake, who in a sense deliberately isolated himself from anything that could be called the experience of his time, and yet saw deeper into it perhaps than anybody. Is there any sort of generalization one can make about the necessity of an involvement in the experience of his time? Let me answer my own question, first, to see what you think about it.

It seems to me it depends entirely on the temperament of the man. If you have a man of a rather active nature and a rather competitive nature, he is bound to want to get involved in his time just to see what things taste like. He may not learn anything by it, but he's bound to want to do it. On the other hand if you have a man who likes the removal of observation and whose wisdom comes from getting triangulations on the sites of action, he isn't going to get himself involved. Do you think you can go beyond that?

VAN DOREN

No, I don't think you can. In other words, there is no formula, I'm sure. There's one thing you didn't mention that makes a poet, and that is his falling in love with the masters. I think there's no question that in the case of Keats, he improved with marvelous celerity from his first work to his last. A lot of that flowed out of his reading with great care the men that he took to be the masters. That's experience to me of a very high order.

It isn't the same experience that most people are having at the moment, because they're not reading those masters. They don't care anything about them. To them they're just names. And yet these poets, like Keats, by digging into these old boys, find things there that they mine and bring out and it's gold for everyone to have. Of course, this is coming back to my theory that poetry is something that reveals and glorifies existence.

MacLeish

But to reveal, one has to have some sort of first-hand apprehension of that which is to be revealed. One of the things that I have found disturbing at various points in my lifetime, and not the least now, is the number of young writers and poets who, in describing the world in which they live, describe a country the existence of which I don't recognize. I don't know what this America is they are talking about. Doubtless it's there and doubtless it's in a particular corner of Greenwich Village or a piece of San Francisco, but it's not this country. It's not New England; it's not the great movement of the continent. I'm not now talking about pessimistic views as against optimistic views. I'm simply talking about a sort of vision of the landscape. I don't know whether you've had this experience, but I keep running into it.

Van Doren

Oh, I often have that feeling, yes. Now, it could be that they have dipped into something that we should know about.

MacLeish

Yes. It may very well be.

VAN DOREN

And if they are good enough they will make us do that.

MACLEISH

Quite. And this is what gives you pause. You wonder.

VAN DOREN

But you know you were really speaking of experience. It's a funny thing, in connection with the poets. Now, take Emily Dickinson. I would say she had all the experiences possible to the human spirit, but she had it in one house and she had it without ever going anywhere.

MACLEISH

Actually in one room, in a part of a house.

VAN DOREN

She happily had been created with an unlimited power to love. I think that she loved everything and everybody, and that sounds silly, but for her it was literally true.

You know, the attempts to name the lover that she rejected were folly, because she loved everybody. She loved women, girls, grasshoppers, birds, flowers and thunderstorms, God and spiders and everything she addressed, including the shadows on the lawn.

MacLeish

Which is perhaps a way of saying that the scope of experience isn't a literal scope; experience can exist in the absolute also. In her case it certainly did. She had the means of exploring the inwardness of her own life to an extent that would have driven you or me absolutely nuts.

Van Doren

Yes. Although to her I don't think she was just burrowing in a hole. To her the world was full of lots of things. It was quite a large world, although it was only the size of this room; yet it had an infinite number of objects in it, none of which was of neutral interest to her. I don't think anything was ever of neutral interest to her.

MacLeish

Those marvelous theological poems of hers in which God becomes whatever it is that the neighbor's dog is barking at over the fence.

Van Doren

Yes. (*Laughs.*) It's a mysterious thing. You know, it's like the attempts to prove that someone else must have written Shakespeare's plays, someone who had had a lot of experience, who had been abroad, who had been to universities and who had been in court. What folly!

MacLeish

Obviously a lawyer.

VAN DOREN

Yes. Think of all the lawyers who couldn't write those plays. Think of all the ambassadors who couldn't write those plays. That's all you have to do. Now, how he knew what he knew I have never known.

I had a student once in my Shakespeare course at Columbia make an appointment with me to talk about something, and he seemed greatly troubled, so I said, "Well, you come tomorrow morning at eleven o'clock when I have office hours." And he came and he said, "You know, it may sound awfully silly, but Shakespeare didn't go to college, did he?" And I said: "Well, I guess he didn't. We really know virtually nothing about him, but yes, I would say it's safe to say that the man who was supposed to be Shakespeare didn't go to college." "But," he said, "how did he know what he knows? He knows more than I do, and I'm taking courses; this course and that course. (*MacLeish laughs.*) It seems to me that I know nothing." I said, "Well, do you think Shakespeare knows a lot?" He said, "He knows everything. How could he do it?" And he started to weep.

MACLEISH

That's touching.

VAN DOREN

That's all there is to it, isn't it?

MacLeish

That's really a very touching story.

Van Doren

Now, what was the knowledge of Shakespeare? It's awfully hard to say. He did not get it by contemplating himself, curiously enough. He contemplated only others.

MacLeish

But then you do get people who you know were deeply involved in historic actions. Wasn't Cervantes supposed to have been very much involved in the armed services?

Van Doren

Yes, he was. And he was a captive of the Moors in Africa.

MacLeish

Who was it who fought at Marathon? Was it Aeschylus?

Van Doren

Yes, I think so.

MacLeish

You don't really get a firsthand account of Marathon anywhere in Aeschylus, nor in Cervantes do you have the real feel of the pike-wielding man. So it's a different kind of experience.

VAN DOREN

> Well, take the case of Cervantes, who had not led a very distinguished life. He wasn't successful at anything. He had written books that didn't succeed. They were books that he had copied from others. He followed certain forms and types, the pastoral and whatnot. And then suddenly with *Don Quixote* it was as if he opened a vein in himself and down, down, down he went with that wonderful stuff that he found down there. It was himself, but it was also you and me or we wouldn't love his masterpiece so much.

MACLEISH

> Now, when you say found a "vein" . . .

VAN DOREN

> Well, I like that word "vein."

MACLEISH

> I like "vein." I don't think it's so much finding it, though. Rather it's a certain obliquity of vision in a given moment which makes experience intelligible to you. Don't you mean the vein was always there? You always knew it was there, but suddenly a knife goes in . . .

VAN DOREN

> And you're able to . . .

MACLEISH

> And you're able to open it?

And you're able to use words that somehow or other assist it to show itself.

They pause.

MACLEISH

Well now, let's take the other side of this relation between man and experience; not that a poet, a good writer, becomes a better poet the deeper his experience, but that the man in experience knows more about his experience, the more he has the qualities and capacities that make a Shakespeare, qualities which Lincoln certainly had.

In other words, would you regard it as a heresy, as a treasonable thing to say, to propose that one of the principal difficulties in our time, in our government, is that those deepest in the experience of the management of contemporary affairs have the least comprehension of what it is they're dealing with?

I think now of the people in charge of the long, laborious undertakings looking toward the prohibition of nuclear arms, the endless debates with the Russians. I'm thinking of Mr. Kennedy's advisers trying to decide what to do with Laos or Cuba, and so forth. You sometimes have a feeling that, although they know all the facts the CIA can give them, and all the facts the records of government can make available to them, they seem sometimes to lack knowledge of what it is they know. You don't regard that as a treasonable observation?

VAN DOREN

No, I certainly don't. They lack what the Shakers used to call the gift to be simple, because there is something very simple there, very clear if we and they could see it.

Now, I think their job is to see it, and help us see it. They're in a position to see it that maybe we're not in. If they could see it, and tell us about it, we could see it too.

MACLEISH

But how in the world is one to bring about this kind of seeing at those levels? Take Cuba; Cuba is an old sad, miserable story. We were wrong. We know we were wrong and everybody involved is sorry, so it isn't necessarily scalping people for the second time to talk about it now. Why did we make that lamentable mistake?

One explanation is that the CIA was badly informed. I'm very willing to believe it was. I think the CIA has proved that it's frequently badly informed, on a purely factual basis. But that wasn't the real difficulty. The real difficulty was that what the CIA thought it knew had no relation to the real situation in Cuba, in terms of the feelings, the commitments, the passions, the anguishes, and the whole internal turmoil of the Cuban people. The CIA was persuaded that a small landing force would raise the people of Cuba, and nothing could have been farther from the truth, because that wasn't the way the people of Cuba felt at that time.

Well now, this is an example, to my mind, of the sort of thing I'm trying to say. Here a great and grievous decision was made by someone who was certainly in the middle of all the experience there was, but who misunderstood the experience because the experience wasn't imaginatively felt. It wasn't felt as human experience. Does this seem to you to be true?

VAN DOREN

It's true, and for me something like that should be true of this thing you call disarmament. The whole world wants disarmament, I'm sure of that. I'm sure there isn't a living soul—oh, there may be a few mad makers of arms for whom this isn't quite true—but I'm sure, on the whole, every living person wants this dreadful accumulation of deadly arms to cease to exist. But nobody seems to know how to do it. There should be some very simple thing to do.

Of course, I have a fantastically childish notion

of what ought to be done. I think we ought to start to disarm. I think it could have the effect that a miracle would have on the whole world.

MacLeish

I wish I could share that conviction, because it sounds so right, and it may very well be right. I wish I could feel the same way, because first of all it would be pleasant to feel that way, and also it would be admirable to feel that way. But what troubles me is that the experience—to get back to that word—of the last twenty years suggests pretty plainly that one is apt to be disappointed if one expects generous actions from the Russians. The Russians at the end of the Second World War had not only promised but they'd explicitly committed themselves to establish democratically representative governments in Eastern Europe. But they didn't hesitate, the moment we disarmed and withdrew, to violate that agreement. They've done this sort of thing so often that one can't help feeling that if we produced a situation in which momentarily the power was entirely in their hands, or permanently in their hands, they would act in a very different way. They would exercise the power they possess. It's very hard not to believe that. And I should think it would be almost impossible for any government in Washington not to believe it.

The thing that troubles me most, Mark, is the fact that short of some such dramatic and trust-

ing high-hearted action as you propose, I don't
see what it is we are going to do.

VAN DOREN

No, I see no way out otherwise, and I'm serious
when I say that. I see no end to the quibbling, and
the so-called negotiation and the arguments and
the backing and filling, which we do too, by the
way. Or at least in the Russian view we do. I
don't know how justified they are in saying so. I
see no hope, particularly as other nations are getting atomic weapons. And they're going to be in
Brazil, I understand, and they're going to be in
France. And maybe they're going to be in Egypt
and Israel in the foreseeable future. I see no escape
other than the miracle of some nation suddenly
having clean hands.

MACLEISH

Well, some nation means either the Russians or
ourselves.

VAN DOREN

Yes.

MACLEISH

And you can be very certain it's not going to be
the Russians.

VAN DOREN

I suppose we can't assume it's going to be us
either. By the way, I'm not saying this is going to

happen. I don't know what's going to happen. I just tremble at the thought of what will probably happen. I'm only saying that if somebody could rise—now here we are talking about poetry again —if someone could rise and speak in absolutely clear tones, and say something like this about this whole thing, so that the whole world would listen, it might make a difference. Think of the revolution that was caused in the history of mankind by Jesus, who asked for nothing; who gave everything away. I suppose no change was ever so great.

MacLeish

The thing that troubles me . . .

Van Doren

Talk about purity of heart, cleanness of mind . . .

MacLeish

The thing that troubles me . . .

Van Doren

Uncompromising!

MacLeish

. . . is not what you're saying, but the argument that is often advanced in support of what you are saying. The argument rests on the proposition that we're faced with the very great likelihood of universal extinguishment of life on the earth. And that faced with that, nothing else matters. At this point I find my gorge rising violently. The whole human development, what has distinguished man from what is not man, has been based throughout history on the willingness of human beings to put what we call principles, to put ideals, to put ideas, ahead of mere safety, ahead of life itself. And down to now we have admired and revered men who risked their lives, gave their lives, and risked not only their lives, but the lives of others with them. Now we find a certain number of people saying—and this is not at all what *you're* saying—that faced with the possibility of the extinguishment of life on the earth, these differences of principle between the Communist conception of what a man is, and the American conception of what a man is, become insignificant. At this point I just resign from the debate.

It seems to me that these distinctions are the important thing so far as the life of the human spirit goes. And that the extinguishment of life—dreadful, horrible, miserable as it would be—isn't necessarily something that by the sheer weight of its horror extinguishes all values.

VAN DOREN

Well, my only notion is that if we can stop this madness—it is a madness that is destroying us, paralyzing us, is making us cease to think, cease to be human; at least I'm afraid it is going to do that, if it hasn't done it already—if we can stop this madness we would restore the very thing you're talking about. Restore a world in which ideas could continue to battle with each other. The battle might be tremendous, intellectually tremendous, but at least no blood would be shed.

MACLEISH

One of the things that concerns you, as it concerns I think most of us, is the fact that with the enormous weight of armament, with all the secrecy that surrounds it, you get a kind of extinguishment of public debate, which means, or may mean—I don't think it has yet happened—which may mean an extinguishment of the individual freedom to have opinions. So that the mere process of defending ourselves, the mere process of preserving our right to have the idealistic views we do have of the nature of man may, ironically, deprive us of those views in action. This, I'd agree, is a dangerous and terrifying thing.

VAN DOREN

I hope, Archie, you understand this; I'm not saying that I want us to survive merely as vegetables, or merely as animals. I want us to survive as men, in some kind of great world court, a world no-man's-land—it might be nothing more than that —able and free to continue to argue, and to reveal to one another what we know, and to be able to conquer with our wisdom, such as it is, the opinion of the world, to bring it into line with our own hopes. That's all I mean. Certainly I agree with you, that the continuation of life . . .

MacLeish

For it's own sake . . .

Van Doren

. . . just as something chemical . . .

MacLeish

Yes.

Van Doren

. . . is of no importance. No, I want to preserve this precious thing that we have built up over centuries. And by "we" I mean everybody, not merely the Americans.

MacLeish

Yes, you are so right.

Van Doren

You know, Archie, we were talking earlier about experience, and death, the experience of death. Now Whitman has suddenly occurred to me. His life is a curious thing to consider. For about thirty years he was an utterly commonplace person. Have you ever read any of his early poems?

MacLeish

No.

Van Doren

They're incredible. They're indistinguishable from the doggerel and drivel that came out of most of the newspaper poets of the time. He was a newspaper man, you know, with a relatively poor education, almost no formal education. But he did have something in him which told him that the two poets who were to be his masters were Homer and Shakespeare, and that's saying a great deal. There's a man who elected masters, by the way. However, that was not until later.

Around his thirtieth year he became silent. We know almost nothing about him for six years, from about 1849 to 1855. He didn't publish anything; we hardly know where he lived. He bummed around, traveled around. It was as if he were in a cocoon. I would say he was sinking, sinking into himself, going down in depth, having the experience that counts.

In 1855 he published *Leaves of Grass,* in which he gave a report of life which wasn't the report that any other American would have given. And as a matter of fact, it was rejected. You know, one copy of that book sold—just one. It had three reviews, two of which he wrote. It was an utter and disastrous failure. And yet, as we all know, in time people did begin to listen.

Many Americans have begun to think that Whitman did give and still does give some kind of true account of what an American can be. But nobody thought so then. Nobody else was thinking that sort of thing then, and yet there was in these poems, in the best of them, a felicity, wouldn't you agree?

MACLEISH

Yes, a marvelous felicity.

VAN DOREN

A marvelous felicity.

MACLEISH

Mark, how about stretching our legs? I'd like to show you where I consult with my muses.

VAN DOREN

A good idea. I've heard you speak of the place through the years. I'd very much like to see it.

MacLeish and Van Doren leave the study and cross the meadows southeast of the main house to MacLeish's fieldstone writing shack. There is no telephone, and it is beyond a determined halloo from the main house. MacLeish sits at a plain writing table. Van Doren sits in a low chair by a window. It is hot under the low roof. They perspire.

VAN DOREN

This is as if I had an appointment with you.

126

MacLeish

> Yes. Well now, Van Doren, what happened to
> you in the examination last Tuesday? What did
> you do good?

Van Doren *(laughs)*
> You know, Archie, this is a very charming room.

MacLeish

> We built this about thirty-two years ago, and I
> have tried various ways of keeping it cool. For
> example, do you see those white lines up there?

Van Doren

> Yes.

MacLeish

> There were panels of building board in there, and
> the mice just loved that. They got in between the
> building boards and the ceiling and they'd run
> races up there.

Van Doren

> So you took the building board out?

MacLeish

> Yes, and it made it hotter, but now that the oak
> tree has grown tall, it's better.

Van Doren

> I know you told me about a cedar, an oak tree,
> and an apple tree. I don't see the apple tree.

127

MacLeish

No, it was cut down. The cedar, I planted; the oak was a volunteer, and the apple tree had been here long before me. I shouldn't have cut it down, but it got so big, sort of thrashing around.

Van Doren

Well, you come here every morning on the whole, don't you? To write?

MacLeish

Every morning.

Van Doren

I remember you did the same thing in Antigua. I remember how you would disappear there and go to a similar structure.

MacLeish

Don't you do the same thing, about eight o'clock?

Van Doren

No, I can't do it that early. I can't get up as early as you do.

MacLeish

You must stay up later.

Mark, tell me a little more about the play that you've just done. You say you've done it half in verse and half in prose. Why did you decide to use verse for part and not for all of it?

128

VAN DOREN

Well, that probably goes back to the Lincoln play in which, of course, I had everybody speak verse except Lincoln. I had him speak prose, on the theory that I would try to make him a better poet in prose than the others were in verse.

MACLEISH

You also used his own language.

VAN DOREN

No, I didn't.

MACLEISH

I thought you did, sometimes.

VAN DOREN

Oh, very seldom. None of his speeches or anything like that. No, it was all dialogue that I made up. And I thought it seemed preposterous to have him speaking verse. By the way, you know, Lincoln tried to write some poems in verse when he was young. Did you ever read them?

MACLEISH

No.

VAN DOREN

Perfectly terrible. But he always had the greatest love of poetry. You know how much he loved Shakespeare and how well he knew it. In any event, in the play I have just completed there are two persons set quite distinctly apart from all the rest of the persons. They are supernatural persons coming into this world of time from the world of eternity, and they go out again at the end. It seemed to me perfectly natural to have them speaking verse, to have them speaking with a kind of formality and a kind of grace which would benefit their origin and their destination. The other persons, who do not believe what they say about themselves, who are a little skeptical or utterly unable to understand what they're doing here, or what they're talking about, these other persons speak prose. Someday I think I'll write a play all in verse, but I haven't done it yet. My third one will be that.

MACLEISH

But you are attracted very much to the theater.

VAN DOREN

Yes.

MACLEISH

And so am I, tremendously. I don't quite understand why, because it is a brutalizing experience.

VAN DOREN

Well, of course I really haven't had your experience in the theater. *Lincoln* was not professionally produced. I know very little about the theater. I wish I knew more. It would be good, I think, for me if I did. The drama, or poetry written in dialogue form—because that's all I mean by drama at the moment—fascinates me. The large amount which it must accomplish in a small space creates fascinating possibilities. You know, a play is a very short thing compared with an epic poem or a novel. *Macbeth,* as you know, is 2,100 lines long; if printed as a novel it would be seventy pages. Just think of all that being accomplished in that space! I don't know of any finer example of compression than that. It's the shortest of Shakespeare's plays. Some people think that it must have been longer once, but a longer *Macbeth* has not been found. I don't miss anything in the one we know.

MacLeish

No, I miss nothing.

Van Doren

And the reason a play must be short is in the very nature of things. It takes a limited number of events happening in a limited amount of stage time, and presses them for meaning—which has to flow finally from outside; the past, or maybe the future or somewhere else.

You know, almost any play, while it's going on, is making the audience think of something that is off the stage. I believe your mind is off the stage as much as it is on.

131

MacLeish

> I hadn't thought of that. I dare say it is true.

Van Doren

> *Hamlet* begins with Hamlet's father already dead. We are being asked to consider the recent death of the father, and then we go back to Hamlet's university friends, Rosencrantz and Guildenstern, back to Yorick who played with him when he was a little boy. . . .

MacLeish

> Back through the actors to the crime itself.

Van Doren

> Yes, and back through the whole of his experience. You see, I would say that about nine-tenths of that play is past. Of course, the supreme example of this is *Oedipus Rex*. All the references in that play are to the past; what the hero once did. That's why a play can be so short.

MacLeish

> I wonder why it is that the dramatic form seems so essential to any attempt to deal with the enormous passions that ravage our lives now. It does seem so to me. I suppose a novel on the scale of *War and Peace* written by a novelist of the stature of Tolstoy could comprehend a great part of what it is that we regard as our own times, but I can't think of a contemporary novel that has even begun to move toward that. O'Neill's plays,

on the other hand, give you a constant sense of
almost opening the door. I don't know what it is
about the dramatic form that seems to have this
sort of consequence, this sort of effect.

VAN DOREN

Well, I wonder if it isn't that the play, by definition, deals with people who find themselves in a
crisis. There is nothing but the crisis. You don't
get ready for a crisis; you have it. A play had
better have it right there in the beginning, hadn't
it? You don't want to monkey around with it;
the crisis must be upon you. And then all that
happens is that somehow or other the crisis is
passed through. Everything works out of the
crisis.

Shakespeare understood this supremely well. You
know Hamlet was the great gentleman of Europe, but as the play proceeds he becomes a
savage. And everyone marvels that this exquisite
gentleman should suddenly have become a brute,
bringing about the death of everybody in the play.

MACLEISH

Perhaps another thing that works in this way is
that on the stage, particularly in a verse play, if
one has the myth in which to work, one doesn't
have the imposition of limits to make real and believable and credible the world which is later going
to turn out to be our world. Instead, one can take a
very limited group of characters who will give you

the fixed points of tension in a situation as you see it, and you can, in a very limited period of time—which, as you say, is the time fixed by the duration of the crisis—comprehend what in a fictional work you'd have to lead up to and lead out of. In other words, I think you are dead right. You can deal with the bare bones of the situation, without all the labors of realization, of the plausible and so forth.

VAN DOREN

And of course you have the supreme advantage that you don't have to talk yourself; you have your people do all the talking. The playwright cannot speak, unless there is a prologue or something of that sort. You remember Aristotle pointed out that that was the difference between a play and an epic poem. In a lyric poem, only the poet speaks; in epic poetry or narrative poetry sometimes the people speak, sometimes the author; in dramatic poetry only the characters speak. There is something clean about dramatic poetry; the characters have to express themselves. And, of course, in the hands of a great playwright they do express themselves; they are all different; they have their own voices, their own styles.

MACLEISH

This play I'm working on now . . .

VAN DOREN

Herakles . . .

MacLeish

Yes, *Herakles*. It seems to have a sort of chronic and recurrent problem that you may be able to give me a little advice on, Doctor.

Van Doren

You mean, I'm a play doctor.

MacLeish

This is a contemporary play in its application, but constructed within the myth of Herakles; that is, the hero, his labors, and the consequences of his labors. It is a play which uses the myth of Herakles as a whole, not simply the Shirt of Nessus and the agony at the end, but the whole myth, the whole story of Herakles.

Van Doren

Well, maybe that's your problem; to squeeze it. Maybe you can't get all of that in—can you?

MacLeish

No, and I don't intend to; not the final episode of the Shirt of Nessus and Herakles' death and so forth and so on.

Van Doren

You mean, that's not germane at all?

MacLeish

That is no part; the thing that makes *The Women of Trachis* is not in it at all.

135

VAN DOREN

I see.

MACLEISH

I really can't say much more about it than that because it still escapes me. I know I've written it
down to a given point three times. The whole
thing is perfectly clear in my mind. Perhaps what
I'm telling you is a piece of psychiatric information rather than a piece of dramatic information.
The play itself is clear in my mind. I know the
actors. I know their relation to each other. I know
the beginning. I know the middle and the end. I
know the application, the implication. But I've
never gotten *to* it. I can begin it. I can move into
the situation. The verse is a four-beat line, like
the line in *JB,* and it works for me; I can write in
it, write easily in it; there's no problem there. But
at a certain point the play simply stops moving
ahead. And I go back and back and back, and try
to get it momentum; and it won't take momentum, you see.

The only explanation I can think of is that, at
some point, somewhere in me I'm not certain
about the feeling of the characters or the myth
they're moving in; whether they conceive of
themselves as innocently in the myth, as any
figure in a myth would be innocently in it, or
whether they're in it without knowing it, without self-consciousness, without any *arrière pensée,*

or whether they are in some way aware of the myth and just a little bit sardonic about it.

VAN DOREN

Yes.

MACLEISH

There's something in the tone there that's wrong. And, as you know certainly as well as I, there's nothing more difficult to deal with than these problems of tone. You can't impose the right tone by saying, "This ought to be the right tone and I'm going to impose it." You don't get the right tone until you begin to feel it.

VAN DOREN

Yes.

MACLEISH

I somehow haven't yet written it. Now in *JB*— I'm an awfully slow writer obviously—*JB* went through many forms before it finally got written. I was bogged down until I conceived Mr. Zuss and Nickles as a pair of circus hangers-on.

VAN DOREN

I see; that came late?

MACLEISH

That came late. And the minute it came, the whole thing fell into place.

137

VAN DOREN

Although, that's how the play begins, isn't it?

MACLEISH

That's how the play begins. It wasn't until I got back to that and constructed the whole beginning of *JB* on that basis that I could use any part of it. Now this is what's wrong with my present play.

VAN DOREN

Incidentally, in *JB*—this is just a parenthesis—in *JB* I remember being terribly hard hit, both in reading the play and in seeing it, by two lines that Nickles, I guess, says: "If God is God, He is not good: if God is good, He is not God." Were they early?

MACLEISH

Yes, they were early.

VAN DOREN

Well, I'm so glad they are there, because that's the whole point, isn't it, about God?

MACLEISH

That little song was always there as Nickles uses it in describing Job's situation.

VAN DOREN

Yes, but you see, what you've got hold of there is the essence of Job, because Job is about the fact that God is not good. God is God.

MacLeish

Yes.

Van Doren

I suppose the simplest fact about God, if I may be presumptuous, is that He's not a good man, He's not a man at all. Is that right? God is not a man; He's God. His power is His attribute, not His goodness.

MacLeish

Exactly, and this is what the whole Book of Job is about.

Van Doren

Of course it's about that. And, by the way, all myths honor this distinction. I mean, the Greek myths do too.

MacLeish

What happens when God appears in a cloud of dust and silences Job? He silences him not by proving to Job that Job is wrong, but by proving to Job that God is powerful and Job isn't. "Where wast thou when I laid the foundations?"

Van Doren

"Who are *you*?"

MacLeish

Yes, "Who *are* you?" "Who *are* you?"

139

VAN DOREN

Well, you raised the fascinating question about the relation between the people in the myth to the fact that they are in a myth. Now, it's such a lovely, lovely problem. Of course, you have to assume that somehow they didn't know. And yet the myth wouldn't have clarity, wouldn't have form and momentum, unless ultimately, somehow or other, they did know.

Now, are you interested in the fact—I think it is a fact—that the figure of Herakles in the Greek imagination, the myth-making imagination, moved from something very serious to something comic? The figure of Herakles almost became the figure of the clown. He *is* a clown, finally, in the *Alcestis* of Euripides.

MacLeish

He is a drunken clown.

VAN DOREN

A drunken clown, a glutton, and so forth. When he goes into the kitchen, he's eating and drinking everything in sight.

MacLeish

Yes.

VAN DOREN

Well, does that interest you?

MacLeish

I'm tremendously interested in exactly that, yes.

Van Doren

Well now, that, I think, might suggest that you permit your people to be sardonic, to have a view both from within and from without.

MacLeish

Yes, that's a very helpful piece of information.

Van Doren

Does it really help?

MacLeish

Yes, it's very helpful. That is very helpful.

Van Doren

Because you know the big strong man, the great man, the powerful man, the man who has his own way in the world because of his strength—just sheer strength—ultimately becomes in anybody's mind a little bit funny, doesn't he? You see, greatness does not consist in that kind of strength. The fact that Lincoln was six feet four is not why we call him a great man, is it? He could have been four feet four.

MacLeish

Also, of course, in Herakles' case, Herakles has such obvious bulk, just sheer bulk; he wasn't only strong; there was a hell of a lot of him.

141

VAN DOREN

Yes.

MACLEISH

And this eventually does turn him into a figure
of fun, but a figure of tragic fun. This is the thing
that is so poignant.

VAN DOREN

Well now, maybe that's not an insuperable difficulty, though I can imagine the difficulty there.
When you say tragic fun, you've got hold of
something that's pretty hard to swing.

MACLEISH

Yes.

VAN DOREN

You have a very large bear.

MACLEISH

This is what I have discovered.

VAN DOREN

Well, far from thinking that you ought to be dis-
couraged, I think you ought to be encouraged by
the dimensions of the bulk.

MACLEISH

I think anything that holds your interest, keeps
your interest, keeps your interest alive, convinces
you that it is potentially exactly what you want

to do in spite of the fact that you can't do it, is infinitely worth doing.

VAN DOREN

Of course it is. Those are the only things that are worth trying.

MACLEISH

I only wish I weren't so slow, Mark.

VAN DOREN

By the way, there's no hurry.

MACLEISH *(laughing)*
Yes, that's a good phrase to remember. I've got to remember that.

VAN DOREN

You know there is no hurry. That's one of the troubles with the world today, Archie. Everybody thinks that something should be done right away. And that's not true. Maybe we could do with a lot of non-doing. Maybe the thing to do now is nothing. But, you know, the journalists and the people who, they say, control public opinion are always calling upon something to be done. I wish we could call a moratorium upon actions for the next ten years; then we might be saved.

MACLEISH

You're a little tired of being told it's later than you think?

143

VAN DOREN

Yes. (*They laugh.*)

MACLEISH

Mark, we began talking a while ago about something else, and I'd like to talk about it a little bit.

You lived in New York through all of your forty-odd years while teaching at Columbia, your years on *The Nation,* even for a while after you left Columbia, which for any writer means, or ostensibly means, living in . . .

VAN DOREN (*laughs*)
Sin.

MACLEISH

Sin; living in literary sin, living in the literary world. But I don't think of you as being part of the literary world of New York. Were you ever part of it?

VAN DOREN

No, I never felt that I was. I sometimes wondered if I shouldn't be, but I didn't know how.

MACLEISH

You mean, you thought it would be a good thing if you were?

VAN DOREN

Well, I thought it might be a good thing practically for me. I think I paid for not being a part of the New York literary world.

MacLeish

You mean, you think it would have been better for you had you been?

Van Doren

I don't know that ultimately it would not have been better.

MacLeish

I doubt it.

Van Doren

Yes, yes. But you know what I mean. Every now and then I saw other people, apparently, reaping advantages out of knowing everybody. You see, Archie, perhaps I had a romantic notion of what the literary life was. If I had such a notion it was a notion of someone living steadily among a population of writers, all of whom talked to one another all the time about what they did and made suggestions to one another and criticized one another's work and helped one another, and so forth, in all sorts of ways, and I know that's essential somewhere in the process. But the fact is, I probably realized that no such thing as the literary life ever did exist.

I did by accident have a few friends who were writers, Allen Tate for one. There was a period in

145

the late 1920's and early thirties when he and I saw a great deal of each other and he was un-exampled in generosity—he loved to read his friend's work. Now, when I say I had writer friends I mean I had friends, but not because they were writers.

MacLeish

So that you would feel fairly dubious about any other sort of literary friendship?

Van Doren

Of course.

MacLeish

I know the only time I had much to do with other writers was in Paris when I was a great deal younger. I certainly did not belong to that group of people Malcolm Cowley calls the expatriates, nor do I think did anybody else. I don't believe anybody thought himself an expatriate.

Nevertheless, I saw a great deal of Hemingway, a great great deal, a good deal of Fitzgerald and a good deal of Dos Passos, but in no one of those cases was this a relationship that had anything to do with their being writers. If anything, the fact that we were all writing was a difficulty, because Scott was an enormous success, Ernest had yet to publish a book, and Dos had published *Three Soldiers*. But nobody knew what was going to happen next, and there was a lot of skittishness on that front.

But the possibility of a literary society on the model of the sort of thing that apparently exists in Bloomsbury or exists in Greenwich Village— or has at one time or another—the possibility of such a society being useful or desirable to any writer, let alone a writer of your dimensions, is to me so minuscule that I can't conceive of it.

VAN DOREN

Well, as I say, I prefer to be glad now that I had excellent friends. I mentioned Allen Tate, and then there was my friend Joe Krutch too, whom I knew as a person long before he ever arrived. Now he's a very successful and well-known writer and an admirable one, but that isn't why I see him. We do read each other's books and all that sort of thing, but still that isn't why we get together.

MACLEISH

Haven't you a sort of an impression, or have you, that writers who have associated themselves deliberately and consciously with other writers in a literary society have really suffered from it? You said that you thought perhaps you paid a price for not belonging to such a society. I wonder if the contrary isn't the case? Although there may be certain advantages to those who do belong to such a society, in the way of reviews and that sort

147

of thing at a given period of time, I wonder if sooner or later they don't lose a great deal; lose themselves, their identities, and become part of the echoes that they hear, part of the shadows that fall across their pages.

VAN DOREN

Now, of course you know there are certain famous examples in the past, either far past or recent past, of writers who did live as a group for a while. There was Jonson's group of poets in the early seventeenth century. Jonson seems to have had a powerful fertilizing influence. Robert Herrick thought Jonson made him, and so did Thomas Carew and all the others, and maybe he did.

Now, I don't think that lasted very long in anybody's case, for Jonson had a kind of stultifying effect. He was a sort of a literary bully. He told people what to do and they did it—of course, he had excellent taste.

In our time John Ransom was such a person down at Vanderbilt University. We've spoken of Allen Tate. Well, Allen would be the first person to say that John Ransom started him off.

MACLEISH

And to an even greater degree I should think Ezra Pound, who during the years when he was in London certainly had a great deal to do with the formation of Eliot, and more to do with the formation of Yeats than most of the admirers of Yeats, of whom I am one, would willingly agree.

But this isn't so much a literary society as it is a series of relationships which proved fruitful in themselves, of themselves. Now, I think one of your great strengths is precisely that fact—that you never have been part of this operation.

VAN DOREN

Thank you, Archie. May I say the same for you?

MacLeish

Oh, you may, with pleasure.

I think the thing to do now is to go have a cocktail and watch the sun go down.

VAN DOREN

Won't the cows come in?

MacLeish

Well, we might shut the door.

MacLeish closes the writing shack door, and then he and Van Doren move along a sickled trail in the high grass, leading to the road and then to the west terrace of the main house. There Van Doren sits facing the sun, MacLeish mixes drinks—a bourbon and water for Van Doren, bourbon with ice for himself. They sit quietly; Van Doren idly creates wet concentric patterns on the top of the terrace table with the bottom of his sweating glass.

VAN DOREN

Have you ever thought, Archie, how large a part mathematics has played in the human experience? As a child, I remember I loved plane geometry and solid geometry. I just loved them. I look upon geometry as a most important part of my experience.

MACLEISH

I look at you with new wonder and awe. You really liked them?

VAN DOREN

Oh yes. Well, of course, I had a very fine teacher who made them exciting. We thought him an old man, but he died just the other day, fifty years after I thought he was a very, very old man.

But you know, Archie, Matthew Arnold, in his talk about the best that's been thought and said, made it very clear that he thought that the great Greek achievements in mathematics and science ought to be part of that. Of course, one of the painful things about this is that I myself am illiterate in science, and I'm not proud of it. With all that's going on today in science as a part of the human enterprise, we ought to be able to communicate with scientists, and they with us.

MacLeish

Well, if scientists will meet you halfway, that is, if they will translate out of their lingo—which they will do sometimes—it isn't difficult to communicate with scientists about scientific problems. Of course, Charles Snow's idea is that there exist two completely different cultures; we're one culture, and they're another culture. But they're not; they come out of our culture.

Van Doren

Of course they do. It's all one at the root. I think Snow was just hoping for more communication between them, such as you see happening by degrees in any university. At Harvard, weren't you occasionally able to talk to a scientist?

MacLeish

Sure. There's a long table in the Harvard Faculty Club, and the most complicated people I know to talk to—mathematicians and physicists and chemists, as well as run-of-the-mill people in other science departments—would quite frequently go there. And when they'd talk to each other, I agree, you couldn't understand what they were saying. They've got a special lingo, and they communicate in terms of signs and symbols, or by a system of references which uses men's names to stand for complicated ideas and conceptions.

But if they were really interested in communicating with you—if George Kistiakowsky, for example, who was Eisenhower's chief scientific adviser, wanted to talk to you—he had no trouble telling you what the nature of the problem was.

VAN DOREN

Well, that was my experience with Polykarp Kusch. Of all things, there's a physicist at Columbia, a Nobel Prize physicist, who bears the name Polykarp Kusch.

MACLEISH

Polykarp Kusch?

VAN DOREN

Yes, P-o-l-y-k-a-r-p, K-u-s-c-h. He is a lovely person. But when he gets to talking with another scientist, say a biologist, you can't understand them either.

MACLEISH

Well, this is true of any so-called discipline.

VAN DOREN

Of course.

MACLEISH

I think you and I could start a conversation without much difficulty that wouldn't be wholly intelligible.

VAN DOREN

Something about anapests.

MacLeish   (*laughing*)
            How are your anapests?

Van Doren

            Or four-beat lines.

MacLeish

            No, I just don't feel this split in life that Snow
            seems to feel. On the other hand, I do know some
            scientists who I sometimes suspect would like me
            to feel there's such a split. Oppy, for example,
            whom I like very much.

Van Doren

            I don't know Oppenheimer.

MacLeish

            Well, he's a lovely person. A beautiful-looking
            person.

Van Doren

            One of the most beautiful faces I've ever seen.

MacLeish

            Sensitive. But he will do this sort of thing. He
            gave the Reith Lecture in London about two or
            three years ago. It was a sort of basic statement
            and description of contemporary physics, hardly
            for the layman, but still for anybody with the
            patience and intelligence to listen. Well, I read
            his lecture, in print, three times. There was
            one paragraph in it that seemed to me to be per-

haps the key to it all. So I learned that paragraph. I learned it. It was hard to learn, but I learned it. It was all in English. There weren't any symbols or anything.

VAN DOREN

I think it's wonderful that you did that.

MACLEISH

Then I met Oppy, and I said, "Oppy, I wish very much you would amplify my understanding of such and such a problem." I tried to put the problem to him. Well, he didn't think I'd put the problem very well, so he didn't want to amplify. Instead he told me a few things he thought I ought to know. And then I said, "But, Oppy . . . ," and I quoted the paragraph from his lecture that I had learned. He said, "Where did you get that?" (*Van Doren laughs.*) He said, "That is the most completely arrant nonsense I've ever heard in my life." "Well," I said, "I think it's a paragraph from your Reith Lecture." Oppy said, "I never heard of it in my life." You know, this is sort of pulling the leg of the victim, and people like Oppy will do that occasionally.

VAN DOREN

You mean, he really had forgotten it?

MACLEISH

No, no. He was having a lot of fun. He knew I

didn't understand it, and he acted accordingly. (*They laugh.*)

VAN DOREN

Well, there's no question, Archie, that mathematics, in its far reaches, is very, very difficult these days. Snow speaks of that, and says he would like communication between scientists and mathematicians and the others; but he says mathematics has become all but impossibly difficult, and he's afraid that this will be a barrier. Nevertheless, he thinks we should still try to smash it.

MACLEISH

Would you say that I am completely wrong in thinking that mathematics is not a general language? It isn't supposed to be a language in which people communicate with each other about the nature of the universe. It's a tool. And the fact that one can't understand all the terms, and doesn't know how to use the tool, doesn't mean that you can't communicate with a mathematician about his translation of what he knows, the substance of what he knows. Does this make any sense?

VAN DOREN

Yes, it does. And I think we should keep trying to do that, trying to make him tell us.

MACLEISH

Certainly, he has got to tell us: *we* can't do it.

155

Not only must the mathematician tell us, but the physicist, the chemist, the astronomer, even the psychologist should translate the lingo of what he knows into a language we can understand. I must say the psychologists have been particularly good about this.

VAN DOREN

Well, perhaps psychology is different. After all, if you take the Greek syllables, psychology is the study of the soul.

MACLEISH

I know. But if you take it from modern practice, it is about the psychological consequences of a series of events, largely sexual. I suppose the soul then becomes a series of reverberations, echoes, I don't know. I don't know what a contemporary psychologist would say the soul was. In any event, psychologists have made a determined effort to communicate what they think they know.

VAN DOREN

Well, perhaps that's because there's a modern assumption that the soul is machinery. It's a materialistic assumption, I would guess.

You know, Archie, we've been studying the mind for a long time now, and it has occurred to me that this has gone along with the fact that we've begun to use our minds less. When we didn't know what the mind was, we just used it and thought. Now that all our attention is upon *how* we think, we're much less interested in *what* we think. For me, what we think is much more important than how we think.

MacLeish

I agree. This raises the question, Mark, can you think of yourself as thinking? Can you sit down and think?

Van Doren

No, I have to be talking to somebody.

MacLeish

And I have to be pounding a typewriter.

Van Doren

Or making notes.

MacLeish

If I am faced with something that I would really like to think about, and I sit down in a chair and say, "Now I am going to think," nothing happens. I think about something else immediately. I have to herd my mind back to the thing I thought I wanted to think about.

Van Doren

I've never caught myself thinking.

MacLeish

I've now reached the conclusion that I'm in-

capable of thought, which is probably not a sur-
prise to anybody except me.

VAN DOREN

No, I reached that conclusion years ago. I used to
drive alone to New York frequently and I would
say to myself, "Well, now, during this two-and-a-
half-hour drive I will think about a given thing."
I would arrive without ever having thought about
it at all. I'd even have forgotten what it was.

MACLEISH

You'd have a poem going in your head, and you'd
say, "Well, during this two hours and a half I'm
going to get it all planned out."

VAN DOREN

All that happened was that those lines kept going over and over in my head.

MACLEISH

I don't think you can make up your mind to
think about a poem, or anything for that matter.

VAN DOREN

Well, perhaps thinking isn't important, at least
not in the way we are speaking of it. For example,
I've often wondered about the incomparable bril-
liance of Democritus, who decided that the world
was composed of atoms. He had never seen one.
He didn't know anything about it, but he decided that the world was nothing but atoms.

Well, by George, he was right: the world is composed of atoms. He's one of those who had inside of himself a little universe, or a big universe.

MacLeish

How do you explain this act of creation?

Van Doren

I don't.

MacLeish

A man puts a name on something he's never seen, which doesn't exist, but actually does.

Van Doren

It actually turns out to be right with Lord Rutherford in the Cambridge laboratories discovering it to be true. Now, that to me is stupendous. I think poetry and mathematics come very close together there, wouldn't you think so?

MacLeish

Well, something and mathematics come close together there; this is a double act of creation.

Van Doren

Oh?

MacLeish

You assert that something exists, the existence of which you can't prove. And then you put a name on it. Naming it is important, creating it is im-

159

portant. Then it turns out, long after you are dead and rotted, that this is true. It isn't really a very satisfactory victory.

VAN DOREN

Well, the reason he was able to arrive at his conclusion was that he wanted to believe that the world was nothing but matter. And those who would say to him . . .

MACLEISH

Do you know that, or do you just assume that?

VAN DOREN

No, I assume so. To those who would ask, "But look, how do you account for the fact that people are individuals, that they're all different from one another, and think and feel in a hundred different ways?" he would reply: "Nevertheless, if you break it all down, ultimately there's nothing but little indivisible things that are boiling around, accidentally assuming shapes. Sure, you're different from him, but it was accident that determined it. You didn't make yourself different."

MACLEISH

A more important question might be: How am I different from that table, if I am different?

VAN DOREN

Well, you are different, but there are atoms in both. (*MacLeish laughs.*)

You see, in order to press this point home, he had to break down everything in his mind to the infinitely small particles of which each thing is composed. It was a stupendous step.

MacLeish

The smallest common denominator of which everything can be constructed.

Van Doren

Right.

MacLeish

It was a stupendous step. The action was tremendous, I agree, and I'm not belittling the action, but what does one know about Democritus? Anything?

Van Doren

Oh, very little, very little. I think there are a few fragments left of him. He was called the laughing philosopher. (*MacLeish laughs.*) I don't quite know why.

MacLeish

Wasn't he third or fourth century B.C.?

Van Doren

Probably a little earlier than that, I would guess. He created the Epicurean school, by the way, which was the human application of his atomic ideas.

MACLEISH

That was the only thing I knew about it.

VAN DOREN

They said, if we're nothing but atoms, why, we'll just live as atoms.

MACLEISH

Let's have the atomic dance.

VAN DOREN

Sure, let tomorrow be what it will. We have no control over anything. We'll just let our atoms dance. And so the Epicurean takes his ease in his garden.

MACLEISH

It gives you that dusty feeling, doesn't it?

VAN DOREN

Yes, it does. And of course the fantastic thing for me is that Lucretius in Rome, a couple of centuries later, or whatever, started all this with such passion. He ought to have been cold-blooded and tight-lipped about it, but he was raging with a fever to convince people that this was true. He wanted to destroy religion with it, you know. "There are no gods. They're just in our minds, which are atoms, which in some cockeyed way produce these illusions, which are also atomic."

MACLEISH

Is it conceivable that two or three thousand years

from now a couple of aged loons will sit under an apple tree, as we're doing now, and talk about our time in which people believed that everything was made of atoms?

Van Doren

They might very well. It might seem very quaint that we thought so.

MacLeish (*laughing*)
I like that.

Van Doren

Well, every now and then, in the history of science and mathematics, as I understand it, there have been great leaps of imagination. This was true of Einstein at the age of thirteen. I understand he began his discoveries as a boy, and as a very young man was promulgating his theories.

MacLeish

Do you know what that nascent, incipient, creative thirteen-year-old hunch was?

Van Doren

No, I don't.

MacLeish

Did it have something to do with the doctrine that later became relativity?

VAN DOREN

Oh yes. That was when he got his first glimpse.
He said so, when he was thirteen. He wrote a
schoolboy paper. His first relativity paper was
published quite early, in his twenties, I think.

MACLEISH

This gives you some really very disturbing insights into what the human mind might turn out
to be, doesn't it?

VAN DOREN

Or take the French chemist Lavoisier, a blazing
genius, who was beheaded, by the way, in the
revolution; he began to think about water once,
and he said: "It may be wrong, what has always
been said about water, namely, that it's a single,
indivisible substance. It may have component
parts." He came out of his laboratory one day
and said it had two parts of hydrogen and one
part of oxygen. I once asked a chemist about him.
And he said, "Well, chemistry has gone a long
way beyond him, but we all admire him very
much. No chemist fails to pay some kind of trib-
ute to Lavoisier. He had something . . . like
intuition."

*MacLeish and Van Doren pause and finish their
drinks slowly.*

MACLEISH

The sky has a sort of hazy, kind of a fuzzy look,

164

as though it might do something very soon, but I don't think it will.

VAN DOREN

Well, it might be cloudy tomorrow.

MACLEISH

I don't believe more than that. Well, I think we probably ought to go in and have dinner, or we'll lose the cook, which is something that I don't care to do.

VAN DOREN

No. When did she expect you, seven o'clock?

MACLEISH

That's right. It's past.

VAN DOREN

Oh well, we can't temporize.

They rise, and move into the house, for dinner and later, sleep.

PART TWO

June 19, 1962

It is warm, and the glaring early mist is everywhere. MacLeish and Van Doren are fresh with sleep, and famished. They breakfast on the east terrace, a belvedere facing a distance, and the Berkshires.

MacLeish

> Would you like oatmeal?

Van Doren

> No, thanks, no. I'm not so much for that.

MacLeish

> Coffee?

Van Doren

> Yes, thank you.

MacLeish

> Mark, now that both of us are retired from teaching—you retired by choice several years ago, while I'm being retired forcefully, legally, for senility in about two weeks, perhaps you can advise me on the use of free time.

169

VAN DOREN

I haven't minded being free of routine. I love to be free of routine.

MACLEISH

Have you been free of routine? Don't you continue to live a life of, not quiet desperation, but quiet discipline?

VAN DOREN

Oh yes.

MACLEISH

You work every morning.

VAN DOREN

Oh yes, but the routine is self-imposed. When I said "routine," I meant one imposed from without. Having to be somewhere at a particular time, having to meet classes. So here we are with the world before us . . .

MACLEISH

How have you used the world since your retirement?

VAN DOREN

Well, I find for one thing that it's very nice occasionally to do nothing at all. That's a lovely thing.

MACLEISH

It's beyond my powers. How have you learned how to do that?

Van Doren

Oh, to let a day just go by, you know; it's a lovely thing, just a day. The day is more important than you are. Sometimes you can appreciate that.

MacLeish

And you watch yourself drift down in the pool of the day.

Van Doren

That's right. Now, of course this doesn't mean that I'm not puttering around on my place, doing things of little consequence. And, of course, I have other things that I do on a kind of schedule. In addition to the writing that I do at home, I go off to read my poems.

MacLeish

Well, you have to support yourself with something.

Van Doren

Yes, that's one of the ways I do it. And I find it very pleasant. I'm asked to lecture sometimes, but I refuse to lecture. I haven't lectured since I left the university. I always say to the people who want me to do this, "I have no subjects." I'm through with subjects.

MacLeish

What do you do with the rest of your life when

you aren't going around supporting yourself by reading your charming poems and talking about them?

VAN DOREN

Well, I stay home. You know Dorothy and I now have only one place, only one residence, and that's our house and farm in Cornwall.

MACLEISH

You gave up the house you lived in in New York when you were teaching at Columbia?

VAN DOREN

Yes, whenever we go to New York, which we have to do occasionally, we stay in a hotel, or sometimes with friends.

MACLEISH

Walk around the city with hayseeds in your hair looking up at the tall buildings.

VAN DOREN

And then we return to Cornwall as soon as we can. My only sorrow is that we can't be there all the time.

MACLEISH

It's been a sort of perpetual friendly and loving conflict between us, whether we're going down there or whether you're coming up here.

VAN DOREN

> Well now, for several years your life has been divided between Harvard and Antigua, that lovely place in the West Indies where we have visited you. Harvard in the fall, Antigua in the spring, then Conway here in the summer.

MACLEISH

> Absolute life of Riley. It couldn't be a more pleasantly arranged life.

VAN DOREN

> To what extent will your life change on retirement? The only difference I can see is that you won't go back to Harvard.

MACLEISH

> I won't go back to Harvard, and of course that means I can stay here through what you and I both agree is the best part of the year, that is September and October, which is the golden month. I suppose October's a golden month anywhere, but particularly here, and early November. But the one thing that I think I will miss somewhat, in fact miss a great deal, is the kind of rather frantic association with the kind of lads you meet at Harvard, and one's colleagues down there. All of them are full of their own problems, and full of ideas and questions, worries, and answers, and all the things that minds ought to be full of. Don't you agree, or do you, that it's a

173

little hard to re-create that kind of relationship on the outside? You go back as an emeritus professor, and you're somebody to whom everyone is very kind.

VAN DOREN

Yes.

MACLEISH

Young men don't quite help you up the steps, but they look sometimes as though they'd like to. And they listen, with half their minds somewhere else, because you're not the fellow who's really going to make very much difference.

VAN DOREN

That's right.

MACLEISH

We're going back to Cambridge this fall for a while, but I don't believe that as a perpetual thing it's going to work out very well.

VAN DOREN

Are you going to be in that lovely apartment that you had in the top of Leverett House?

MACLEISH

Yes, Harvard put us ten stories up, looking down on the Charles, you remember? Actually, you were going to be there once yourself.

VAN DOREN

Well, I remember it for the simple reason that it makes me rejoice to think that next spring we'll be there too, in that same apartment. You don't really mind this?

MACLEISH

Oh, I love it. My goodness, this is one of the finest things that every happened.

VAN DOREN

Well, I've been asked to go lots of places for a term, but I've never wanted to do it. But I couldn't resist this.

MACLEISH

I'm glad you couldn't resist it, because they've wanted you up there so long. If you can accomplish this sort of sedentary heaven you're describing, in which you will travel as little as possible and stay put, and occasionally just let a day go by, you're going to become the sage of the Connecticut woodland.

VAN DOREN

Well, Archie, to me one of the most important jobs a person has to learn is how to live with monotony. I love monotony; I love day after day without radical change. Every day is a little bit different from every other. And finally you can come to appreciate those little differences; they become huge differences.

MACLEISH

The more I get to know about you, the more remarkable you are to me. The one thing I can't
bear is monotony.

VAN DOREN

Really?

MACLEISH

Drives me absolutely crazy.

VAN DOREN

I just live on it.

MACLEISH

Well, maybe I don't know what you mean by
monotony. The repetition of a pattern, yes, I
love that, and I love having a day that follows
the pattern of other days, so that you work
mornings . . .

VAN DOREN

Yes.

MACLEISH

. . . you do some work around the place, you
eat lunch, then you go out and dig in the garden,
you take a swim, you read, you have a couple of
good cocktails, you have dinner and you putter
around a while and go to bed. Now, if that's what
you mean by monotony, I adore it. But if you
mean just one . . .

VAN DOREN

One tone?

MACLEISH

Yes, one tone.

VAN DOREN

That's not the word, I suppose. At least I didn't mean one *gray* tone. No, I meant repetition.

MACLEISH

Kierkegaard has a book on monotony.

VAN DOREN

A book on repetition. He suggests that the art of living is the art of coming to terms with repetition, because all life is repetition. Not only do the generations repeat one another, not only do all people do the same things on and on and on forever, but in every given life there must be repetition; three meals a day, breakfast every morning, oatmeal for you.

MACLEISH

Aha. Yes.

VAN DOREN

Do you get tired of oatmeal?

MACLEISH

Not a bit. I thank God that I don't get tired of breakfast.

VAN DOREN

What would a person be like who said: "I will change my life. I will not eat breakfast"?

MACLEISH

Well, a man could do that. He'd probably end up in an institution sooner or later if he did. But doesn't the stitching of the monotony, the repetition of the stitch have to have pattern in it in order to be habitable?

VAN DOREN

Oh yes. Well, pattern comes in inevitably because even if you tried to make your life all one thing you couldn't keep it that way. Things are always happening. Accidents happen, and new people come into your life. You read something that amazes you. You get ideas that you didn't have yesterday, of course. But those things are important only when they break the circle that is there. The circle must always be there to be broken.

MACLEISH

Isn't there also this experience? At least I think I've had it: you feel that you've hit on something that you've never quite hit on before, something very exciting, something excitingly new, something creatively new. And then you work on it. You give this thing shape and then you begin to look over some old notebooks some rainy afternoon and you find out you thought just exactly the same thing when you were twenty-four. But it didn't hit you then.

VAN DOREN

Yes.

MACLEISH

You wrote it down but it didn't hit you, so that sometimes it suddenly occurs to you that the process of learning is the process of discovering really to be true what at the beginning they told you was true, but you didn't quite capture it then.

VAN DOREN

Well now, that to me is a justification of monotony or repetition, if you please. What is ritual? Men live by ritual. Without ritual we would not have human life, I think. You see, we could eat just by grabbing something and stuffing it in our mouths as we walked along. But we come to a table. We sit down. We have things there that have been put before us.

We use tools, silver tools that have been given to us, and we talk while we eat. We make a ritual out of eating. What is marriage, what is a wedding, except a ritual? It's a statement to all concerned that these two people are going to live together. They could just begin to live together, but for some reason or another people want to have it said publicly.

What is a funeral except the statement: "This man has died"? You don't just drag him off.

MacLeish

Yes. You don't just put him underground. The ritual statement there is one that throws a lot of light on the way our minds work, it seems to me, because it gives dignity backward. Here is this inert piece of mud which is shortly going to stink, but it was a man, and the ritual looks back over the life of the man. Even in the life of a very mediocre human being it somehow or other contributes largeness, not because anything has changed, but because the attitude, the minds that look back on the man's life give it size. He becomes a man, a man who has suffered the human fate.

Van Doren

And the habit that people have of collecting when one of their friends dies to talk about him, or to think about him, is a very good habit, because suddenly they see him as they never were able to see him before. They never really saw him before because he was always changing. Now he's stopped changing; and there he is in outline. There he is stamped on their minds somehow or other, and they're able to say: "Well, he was such and such a kind of man. After all, we didn't know it, but that's the kind of man he was."

MacLeish

Did you know Edward Pickman?

Van Doren

No.

MacLeish

Well, he was one of those New England characters. He was a man who wanted to be an historian of ideas, and made a very good start at it, beginning a long series of books.

He was married to a devout Catholic, Hester Pickman. His children, obviously, were all Catholics. But he himself maintained his Unitarian seclusion, and when they came to bury Pick the problem was raised as to what to do with a man who lived surrounded by faith, but had himself existed in a considerable degree of skepticism.

So they held a funeral in a little church in Bedford, and they had a period of silence. Nothing happened. People just sat there. Many of the people who sat there were so embarrassed by the silence that they talked about it for years afterwards. But a few people felt that this was exactly the appropriate way to deal with a man who had refused to become part of an organization of

thought, but who had just been himself, and re-
mained himself and had died himself.

VAN DOREN

And he became himself more at that moment
than he ever had been before, at least in the
minds of the others.

Well, think of all the ways that we ritualize
things. For instance, the process of learning could
go on informally with us all. We could just begin to learn. We could find books to read, and
so forth. But we set up colleges and universities
which ring bells at nine o'clock in the morning,
and the students go into certain rooms to study
certain things, and they do that for so many
weeks, and then they take examinations. Unless
we formalize and ritualize things, it seems to me
we'd never get anywhere.

MACLEISH

Well, certainly this formalization has a great deal
to do with the possibility of marriage and the
loveliness of marriage. One of the things that
bores me most is the recurring assumption, which
lies at the back of most romantic novels, that
marriage becomes stale and old and tired because
it's the same woman and it's the same bed and
it's the same night, and it goes on and on. But,
heavens, this is what life is. This is what marriage is all about: the continuation of the excitement of the meeting, the recognition, those con-

stantly renewed recognitions which are always a
little different, but always the same.

Incidentally, you and I have two of the only really
permanent marriages in America. They ought to
be visited like holy shrines.

VAN DOREN

Yes, we've been very lucky.

MACLEISH

I think we've been reasonably lucky, but wouldn't
you say we've contributed to our own good for-
tune? (*They both laugh.*) But really they *are*
marvelous edifices.

VAN DOREN

You know, Archie, in marriage there's novelty
every moment; but it can be measured against
something that doesn't change.

Strangely enough, James Thurber believed this
with all his heart. You might not assume he
would, but poor old Jim, who died not long ago,
used to talk with great passion about how the
love of one woman was more like love than the
love of many women. He couldn't always explain
it, but he was perfectly sure about it. He was sure
there was more novelty, more change, that way.

MACLEISH

That does come oddly; not oddly from Thurber,

I'm sure, but oddly from one's preconceptions as to what sort of man Thurber was. But I think it's completely true, and one of the sad things is that so few people ever have an opportunity to find that out.

VAN DOREN

Yes. Jim Thurber was, as you know, one of the funniest men in the world, but he was also a very serious man.

MACLEISH

He'd been a very dear friend of yours for many, many years, hadn't he?

VAN DOREN

Many years. More than twenty years.

MACLEISH

I still remember Jim's remarks at the ceremonial they held for you at Columbia when you retired.

VAN DOREN

Yes, they were wonderful.

MACLEISH

Wonderful human affections.

VAN DOREN

Well, there was something that was always in Jim's mind, and I never knew what to do about it. I wanted him to forget it but he never would.

184

It had to do with the first time I met him. Did I ever tell you about that?

MacLeish

No.

Van Doren

It was in 1941 at Martha's Vineyard. Jim had just had the last of five operations on his remaining good eye. You know, when he was a boy one eye had been shot out by his brother with an arrow, a thing that happens appallingly often among children.

His brother had said, "You go up there and stand with your back to me, and I'll shoot you in the back and see if it hurts." The arrow wasn't much; a little wooden thing. Well, Jim stood there a long time and the arrow didn't come, so he turned around to see why it wasn't coming, and it was coming.

That was when he was a child. So he had only one good eye. But now, in the late thirties and around 1940 the other eye began to have a cataract which couldn't be fixed. He had had the fifth and final operation, and they couldn't do any more. He was substantially blind.

That evening when I first met him on the beach at Martha's Vineyard there was a party, and nothing much was said. But the next afternoon

185

he arrived at the house where we were staying and said he wanted to see me. That surprised me. I didn't know what he wanted to see me for, but he said: "I want to see you alone. Let's go out on the side of the house and talk."

So we went out—I led him out—and we found chairs and we sat down, and I looked at him and he was weeping. Tears were literally running down his face, and I said, "What's the matter, Mr. Thurber?" He said: "This is a punishment. This blindness is a punishment." I said: "Why? What for? How could it be a punishment?"

He said: "Well, in my writings I have always dealt with meanness and stupidity. My subject has never been goodness and strength. I have always talked about poor, weak people. I made fun of them. So this is a punishment. I have been stricken blind."

Think of a man like that thinking such a thing. But he really did think it. Well, I had to think fast myself. And I said what anyone might have said. I said: "You know, Mr. Thurber, everyone who's ever read you knows that you are for goodness and strength. But you deal with it in reverse, so to speak. You are a satirist and you deal with the opposites of goodness and strength in order to reveal your true belief." He said I'd saved his life. He never forgot that, and he al-

ways thought of me—in a way it was embarrass-
ing—he always thought of me as a kind of oracle.

MacLeish

Well, Mark, he's not the only one who's thought
that about you.

Van Doren

But anybody could have said that.

MacLeish

Anybody could but nobody did.

Van Doren

This shows, by the way, how serious a man he
was.

MacLeish

It also shows something else. It shows that perhaps the best and most powerful way to expose
the goodness of goodness, the power of love, is to
surround it with its grotesque opposites, because
I share your feeling. The one thing, long before
I ever met Thurber, the one thing I felt about
him was that this was a man with a deeply comic
or, put another way, a deeply enveloping understanding of the wonder of being a human being,
and the miracle of being men and women. Why
in the world divide up this way, you know? This
came out of his work.

What happened when Jim died?

VAN DOREN

Well, Jim's last summer was a bad summer for him. Nobody knew what was the trouble. He was very unhappy and irascible, and people thought he was being sort of ornery, but actually he had a brain tumor and was, I suppose, under very great pressures of every sort. Well, he died and was taken to Columbus, Ohio, where he was born. He was buried there very simply. I don't think there was a true funeral.

MACLEISH

Yes. I wondered if there was.

VAN DOREN

In the future there may be something like a memorial.

MACLEISH

There never was a memorial service?

VAN DOREN

No.

MACLEISH

There ought to be.

VAN DOREN

Yes, there ought to be. Still, he did have a kind of memorial when he died; people all over the world wrote about him and thought about him and talked about him.

MACLEISH

How do you account for the universality of his
appeal to the conscience and sensibility of his
time? Do you suppose the comic language, the
language of comedy, of tragicomedy is the most
universal language?

You know, the language of tragedy can also be
universal in its purest form, but it tends to deal
with specific situations and specific countries.
Whereas Thurber's vocabulary, or the alphabet
in which he wrote or drew, was an alphabet that
anyone anywhere could understand.

VAN DOREN

Of course, the curious thing about a great come-
dian like that is that the things he says which
make you laugh are not necessarily funny for
him. When Jim stated the appalling discrepancies
and inconsistencies, the cockeyed impossibilities
of life, he revealed to you that they can present
themselves that way—just head on. He would
speak of these things in a way that you had never
thought of them before, although he had been
thinking about them all of his life. You would
laugh, but he was quite serious.

Mark Twain was that way, you know. At the
end of his life he was troubled because some of
the most dreadful things that he'd said and believed were laughed at.

189

Ada MacLeish speaks from behind the screen door, asking if MacLeish and Van Doren will take the station wagon and pick up an order she has placed at the Conway grocery store. MacLeish and Van Doren agree, and go off.

Later MacLeish and Van Doren return from Conway and take the baskets and cartons of groceries into the kitchen. They return to the west terrace and sprawl out on deck chairs under an ample apple tree. They study the fields sloping up and away to the horizon.

VAN DOREN

It's nice the way the land there rises continuously.

MACLEISH

Yes, there's a constant rising, when you walk there, as you go up that hill.

VAN DOREN

Archie, your motto must be "Excelsior." Incidentally, do you know A. E. Housman's parody of Longfellow's "Excelsior"?

MACLEISH

No.

VAN DOREN

You know, Housman was a wicked parodist, a devil in his own way:

"The shades of night were falling fast,
    The snow was falling faster,
    When through an Alpine village passed,
    An Alpine village pastor."

MacLeish   (*laughing*)
            Oh, that's beautiful.

Van Doren
            Well, you know, he was always taking off things.

MacLeish   (*laughing*)
            "Through an Alpine village passed, An Alpine
            village pastor." It kills me.

Van Doren
            It takes genius to find something as simple as that.

MacLeish
            Well, that's just wonderful.

            They pause, chuckling; and then:

MacLeish
            Mark, have you any plans to use your free time
            to travel, that is, beyond going around reading
            your poems?

Van Doren
            No, traveling for its own sake doesn't really in-
            terest me. I now move about a little more than
            I want to, although I'm not too sure of that, be-

cause I'm always glad to go as I am glad to come home. Have you got any theories about travel as such? Are you a traveler?

MACLEISH

I've got strong feelings about travel. I don't believe I am, by impulse, a traveler, because I detest living in hotels, for one thing; and living in hotels is a condition of traveling. That is, unless you can arrange to get yourself aboard a ship that's going to go to various places, and stay bedded down there.

VAN DOREN

Well, that's a floating hotel.

MACLEISH

Yes, that's a floating hotel, but somehow it's different. The important thing about travel is that a change of scene, a very considerable change of scene, a movement from one continent, culture, language, and so forth, to another, produces a change in the perspective or the habit of viewing in a way that can renew your excitement about your own experience of the world. This is particularly true if you go to a city that you love, as Ada and I love Paris. You know, Ada and I, during our late twenties and early thirties, lived there for six years.

VAN DOREN

You lived there that long?

MACLEISH

Oh yes, and you know today, although Paris is very much changed in many ways, it remains fundamentally the same, and it continues to alter my feelings about myself. I can sort of see myself as a younger man moving around in Paris, and I build on those conceptions, and start all over again.

Or take Persia, where I spent five or six months when I was fairly young. This is, without doubt, a radical and revolutionary change of scene. You're up eight, ten thousand feet on the high plateau of Persia. You're in an arid, impoverished, forbidding, and incredibly beautiful land, where men live in isolation behind their earthwalls with overhanging peach boughs. That's the great symbol of Persia, the peach bough over the mud wall.

VAN DOREN

Yes.

MACLEISH

This kind of experience picks you up and puts you down again. So for a man working, a man writing, it seems to me that travel is terribly important.

But just add one more thing to that; one of the things that worries me about some youngsters I've known, some young writers I've known as students, is the apparent feeling that they can only

193

write outside their own country. The general exodus, recently to Rome, and before to Paris—it has been to Spain—a good deal to Mexico—is, I think, a self-deluding attempt to solve one's problems as a writer by going and living somewhere else. Don't you think so?

VAN DOREN

Oh, I'm sure of it. I would not call myself a traveler. Travel is never an end in itself. There are people, you know, who couldn't live unless they were going somewhere all the time.

MACLEISH

Dos Passos.

VAN DOREN

Uh-hum.

MACLEISH

Don Passos cannot stay put. He's a perpetual, perennial traveler. His foot itches.

VAN DOREN

Well, that's at one extreme. I know other persons whose names you wouldn't know, who are so restless that every season—maybe three or four times a year—they're off somewhere. And when they come back, it seems to me, they're not the slightest bit changed. They live in hotels, they see the things they're supposed to see, and I'm sure they find all these places very much the same. All they've done, that I can see, is to avoid what for them is the boredom of staying at home. I pity anyone who's bored by being at home.

MacLeish

Well, don't you pity *anyone* who's bored?

Van Doren

Of course I do.

MacLeish

Have you ever been bored? Can you remember a time you've been bored?

Van Doren

I hope not.

MacLeish

I've been bored by myself. I myself bores me. (*Van Doren laughs.*) But I've never been bored by where I myself was.

Van Doren

The person who can't stay anywhere might as well be nowhere. And, of course, it's a mistake too for a person never to leave home. You remember how the *Two Gentlemen of Verona* begins: one gentleman is saying to another, and they're speaking of their young sons, one of whom has gone away on the Grand Tour of Europe, "Home-keeping youths have ever homely wits."

MacLeish   (*laughing*)
            I'd forgotten that.

Van Doren

            "Homekeeping youths have ever homely wits."
            Of course we must get away! Now, although I
            don't believe in traveling, I do not regret any bit
            of traveling I ever did. On the contrary, when I
            was there, it was unspeakably wonderful.

MacLeish

            You know, Mark, one can avoid home in the
            sense of "homekeeping youths" in the way that
            Thoreau did. How far is Walden Pond from
            Concord? Two or three miles?

Van Doren

            Not that much, no.

MacLeish

            Well, you can hardly get the car in third gear
            before you're there. And yet for Thoreau this was
            a movement into another world. And this, after
            all, is the really essential thing about travel. Not
            that you learn anything about other people by
            seeing them elsewhere, but that you learn a lot
            about yourself—if you have the curiosity.

Van Doren

            My two or three residences in England are very
            important to me. And in France. And then a few

years ago in Greece. I'm certainly glad I went there.

MacLeish

This Greek thing meant a great deal?

Van Doren

Oh yes.

MacLeish

I remember your talking about it. I don't know why I remember it, but I do remember your telling me about a meal on the sidewalk of a road going through a little village. There was no place to eat, so people brought a table out and you ate on the street of the tiny village. And suddenly, you were in the life of the town.

Van Doren

Yes, we were in a car and going over the mountains down into Arcadia.

MacLeish

"Over the mountains, down into Arcadia." What a remarkable thing to say.

Van Doren

Well, something went wrong with the car. The mountain roads had caused the radiator to boil up and it sprang a leak. So we got out, turned the car around, and pushed it to a little village where there was a blacksmith shop. The blacksmith had some solder and could fix the radiator, and he did that. But while we were waiting to have this done, we walked up and down the village street. There was only one street, and as a matter of fact, the houses were only on one side, because the other side fell off. It was on one of those great declivities.

Well, we were hungry, so we went into a little shop and bought bread and cheese and wine. But we had no place to sit down and eat it. So we laughed and said—there were four of us, Dorothy and I and two friends—we said, "Well, we'll just walk up and down the street of this town eating. We don't care what people think."

At that very moment a door opened, and we saw a man coming out backwards, and then we saw that he was carrying one end of a little table, a sort of a kitchen table. At the other end was another man. They were bringing this table out for us. They couldn't speak a word to us, nor we a word to them, but they knew that we wanted to sit down and eat.

So they put the table in the middle of this little street, and one of the wives of these men came running out with a roll of paper. It was old, dirty paper, but she spread that out, like a cloth.

MacLeish

Yes.

VAN DOREN

Then they brought chairs, rickety chairs. It was an unspeakably poor village. And they bowed to us and asked us to sit. Then the whole village stood around and watched us eat.

MACLEISH

It's strange, but my two visits to Greece had the same powerful effect on me that Greece had on you. The thing I also best remember is a meal. We were invited to go out with George Seferis, the Greek poet, who is now the Greek Ambassador in London. Incidentally, I think he's a really marvelous poet.

VAN DOREN

Yes, he is.

MACLEISH

Well, we were with Seferis and a man who is known in Athens as the Colossus of Rhodes. I think his name is Katsimbalis, a great vociferous man. And there were a number of other people. We were taken out to the village where—who was the orator who put pebbles in his mouth?

VAN DOREN

Demosthenes.

MACLEISH

Demosthenes. The village where Demosthenes was born, on the other side of Mount Hymettus.

I remember it was a cold spring morning; a table was put under budding vines, and then, in the Greek manner, all sorts of hors d'œuvres were served, one after the other, and wine, that resinated wine.

Finally, at the end of a repast which looked as though it were going to leave us hungry, but instead left us absolutely replete, I said to Seferis: "Here we are under Mount Hymettus. I don't understand Greek, but I'd love to hear one of your poems in Greek. Would you read one of your poems?" And Seferis said, "No, I won't. I don't remember my own poems." And he made excuses. Whereupon Katsimbalis said, "It just so happens that I have in my pocket . . ." (*Van Doren laughs*) and he pulled out a new poem by Seferis, and he read it in Greek. Well, I sat there looking up at the pure line of Hymettus; and I really thought myself in the elsewhere that is holy. Do you know what I mean?

VAN DOREN

Of course.

MACLEISH

I didn't have the remotest idea what any of the words meant, but the sounds enchanted me.

VAN DOREN

I remember once on Crete we had seen what there was left of the palace at Knossos, and our driver was taking us inland. Well, it came noon and we were all hungry and thirsty. There were vineyards there, so the driver went off and brought bunches of grapes from them, and we ate them; and he said it was all right to do that. Then he said, "I think there's a little house down here by a stream where we can get lunch." Well, we got to this place. The stream was dry, just as dry as a pavement. Of course, it had water in it only a few weeks of the year.

MacLeish

A torrent, I'll bet.

Van Doren

Well, we crossed the little bridge, and there, under a huge plane tree, which the old man who lived there said was five hundred years old, we were asked to sit down. And out came the old man and his wife, the old wife in a black gown or dress clear to the ground, and the old man hobbling with a stick. They asked us to sit down, and they said they would give us lunch.

First, the old wife brought out four little glasses and put cold water in them from a little spiggot that she had nearby, and rubbed them with her hands to get them good and clean.

MacLeish   (laughing)
Yes.

VAN DOREN

She then poured the wine. She left us, and then eventually returned, bearing a little tray on which were four dishes full of the most delicious stew of some sort that I have ever eaten in my life. As a matter of fact, we were a little bit worried because you know what can happen to you from eating . . .

MACLEISH

Yes.

VAN DOREN

. . . food in Greece. But we looked at one another and said we would eat this if it killed us.

MACLEISH (*laughing*)
Yes.

VAN DOREN

As a matter of fact, it made us well. Well, as soon as we and the driver were through, we started off. And I said to the driver: "You know they did consent to take a little money for the lunch: I was afraid they wouldn't. How did they happen to have this delicious stuff there to eat? They didn't have time to prepare it." He said: "It was their lunch. It was their dinner." That was their main meal, but they had let us have it. And the fact that they had sold it wasn't the significant thing: they let us have it.

MACLEISH

Yes, they let you have it. This reminds me about
a time in the Aegean a couple of years ago when
we decided to land on the east side of an island
that almost nobody goes to called Eos.

VAN DOREN

Oh yes, ordinarily you would go to the west
side of it.

MACLEISH

Yes, where the town is. But we landed on the east
side because of a very strong unusual westerly
wind. We went ashore, and there was a little
group of houses on a great, arid, dry, burned
landscape full of goats. We walked up a sort of
little narrow road between the walls, and suddenly there came a flock of goats, driven by a man
on a burro who obviously was the owner. He drove
down through his goats. He bowed to us. And
then he put his hand into the bosom of his shirt
and he brought out a handful of white stuff,
which appeared to be a kind of cottage cheese.
(*Van Doren laughs.*) And we were expected to
eat it. And I thought: How does one do this?

VAN DOREN

Yes?

MACLEISH

Well, we did it.

VAN DOREN

You dipped it with your fingers?

MACLEISH

It was warm with his body. We dipped our fingers into his hand and we ate it. And then he gave us pieces of a great loaf of the most beautiful brown bread. This was our welcome, a welcome to his beach, to his coast, his land. It was simply wonderful.

VAN DOREN

It reminds you that hospitality was the Greek religion, in a sense.

MACLEISH

And that the quality of Greece, in the farms, out in the islands, down in the Peloponnesus, is not at all the quality of Athens.

VAN DOREN

No.

MACLEISH

It's a wonderfully rich, warm, and hospitable quality.

VAN DOREN

I'll always remember another instance. We were through looking at Crete, for our purposes, and we were back in Heraklion, waiting to take the plane back to Athens. I had come downstairs first,

and the rest of the party was upstairs. I was standing alone and tired and hot on a dusty street. I
was thinking to myself: I'm awfully tired. I wish
they'd come down. But they didn't come. So I
said, "I wish I could sit down." At that very moment I felt a tap on my shoulder; and there was a
little boy with a chair. (*MacLeish laughs.*) He
had seen this old man—that's me—who looked
tired, and he had come out of a . . .

MACLEISH

I don't believe it for a minute. If I ever saw a man
who didn't look either old or tired, it's you. He
probably just thought you needed a chair.

VAN DOREN

He had come out of a little shop with this chair.
It almost collapsed under me; it had no strength
to it. And then I made a bad mistake. I'm
ashamed of this; I reached in my hand for a
drachma. He said, "No." He wouldn't let me.

MACLEISH

In Greece the other hand is not out for bakshish.
They're people of a dignity, a nobility. I think
Greece is the best of all the great restoring countries, and the countries that give you a sense that
the world still has value and richness in it.

You know, Mark, all these things we've been
recalling from our travels have to do with the
restoration of one's own sense of the value of hu-

205

man associations. Americans still think they're the most generous and friendly people in the world, but these graces one finds in Greece, these small gestures that give sense to life, we've forgotten about most of those.

VAN DOREN

As a matter of fact, we tend to be suspicious of strangers, whereas for them, it was a religion to honor strangers, to be good to strangers, to be hospitable.

MACLEISH

The Greek dream. You know, Mark, we in America may not honor strangers, but we have a dream of our own, the dream we were talking about on the way up from the village this morning. Where did the American dream come from, if not Greece? Not from our own landscape certainly. I can't help believe that the American dream to the first settlers was a nightmare.

VAN DOREN

It was not a dream.

MACLEISH

It was not a dream, it was a nightmare. They were surrounded by danger. The trees were their enemies. They had to cut, hew, break up, pull out roots. Stones were their enemies. The Indians were their enemies. And it was a brutal and bitter struggle. I suppose there was hope, hope of making a good living. Certainly in New England agriculture did provide a good living well down to the beginning of the last century, well down to the opening of the West.

VAN DOREN

Yes.

MACLEISH

But where does the American dream begin, Mark? Do you have to wait for Jefferson? Is it as late as that?

VAN DOREN

I would think so. You have to wait until the vision extended almost indefinitely West, and you thought of the country as something that was going to be huge.

MACLEISH

When you knew you could master the land, when you moved out into the prairies, when you moved into the high lands, the high plains, when you went over the mountains and into California, it was then that the dream began to become promise. Isn't that it?

VAN DOREN

Yes, I believe so.

MACLEISH

Well, if that's true, then it raises a very interesting question about the concept of America now. If the American dream is related—as some sardonic historians say—to the material possibilities of the opening of the continent, what happens to it now that the continent is fully occupied? Does the sense of promise die with the hope of material fulfillment, or is there still that thing that Lincoln talked about when he said that the essence of the Declaration of Independence was that it gave all men everywhere the hope that the weights would some day be lifted from their shoulders? Have we lost that, or haven't we? I think that's the most grievous question that men of our generation have to face.

VAN DOREN

Well, you know, I often wonder what it means now to say that we should love our country. I certainly think we should.

MACLEISH

You know that you do.

VAN DOREN

Yes, I know I do, and maybe everybody does, but it's a very different thing from what it used to be.

MACLEISH

Exactly! What is this object you love?

VAN DOREN

Is it a single thing?

MacLEISH

Yes, is it a single thing?

VAN DOREN

I think it has to remain single. You know I often look back with a certain kind of nostalgia to Greece of the fifth century. I get the impression that every young Greek knew what he lived in. He was born into a going thing. He knew what it was. Maybe he couldn't find words for it, but he was proud to belong to it, was prepared to make any sacrifice to perpetuate it. And I'd say, Archie, that the same is true here now. You see it during our national party conventions. Here are the delegates from the various states, getting up and bellowing forth their identifications: "the great State of Montana," "the great State of Florida," "the great State of Georgia," "the great State of Illinois." All of them are assuming, are they not, that there's one thing here with fifty parts. There's no assumption that it isn't one thing.

MacLEISH

Then, the possibility of the breaking up of this whole is no longer a real possibility, it's no longer conceivable in anybody's mind?

VAN DOREN

I think not.

MacLEISH

But still, if the country is more firmly than ever

before an economic, an industrial, a political whole, is it creatively *itself*? Does it have the kind of impulse it had at the time of the early settlers—that America is the beginning of the future, that the future *is* America?

VAN DOREN

Yes, I would think so.

MACLEISH

Does it still have a central idea? You know, Mark, there's only one central idea, that ever was America, as I see it. That central idea was human freedom. It is the idea that all men are created equal, an idea which the wiseacres have sneered at and laughed at for so long: "Of course, they're not created equal." But of course they are! I continue to hold that this central idea is the only idea that ever was America, but I ask to what extent is it still an American idea?

During the McCarthy time, for example, it seemed to me that a great part of the country was frightened, including the so-called conservatives and particularly the well-to-do. And a great part of the country was thus lost to this central idea which is America. They were trying to build walls around what they had, instead of opening out the fences toward freedom. What that situation is now is anybody's guess. I can't help believing that the idea of freedom still exists.

Van Doren

Neither can I.

MacLeish

The difficulty is how to measure to what extent it still exists. How can anybody know the temper of America? Usually when you have somebody reporting on the temper of America in the *New York Times Magazine,* which is a good reporter on the temper of America, or when you have somebody reporting through various forms of testing, samples, averages, and so forth, usually what you have is a mathematical attempt to find out what it is that people think. For example, you get reporters moving around before an election, talking to political leaders here, there, and elsewhere. Then they tell you that Kennedy is going to win or Nixon is going to win.

Van Doren

Or, as they say, a sampling; they've taken a sampling.

MacLeish

Yes, yes. Or you have professional opinion samplers, people who have made a reputation out of their ability to do this. Do any of their findings persuade you? Are you persuaded, are you convinced, that you are really listening to an account of, a representation of, the temper of America?

Van Doren

No, because they've never asked me.

MacLeish   (*laughing*)

                If they did ask you, would you think so?

Van Doren

                Well, I would tell them.

MacLeish

                You'd tell them what you think, but . . .

Van Doren

                What my answer means, is that they have to ask everybody before they know.

MacLeish

                But even if they asked everybody, would a mathematical summary, so many *yeses* and so many *noes,* give you the answer?

                I do think that when you're talking about the temper of a country, which means not only how people are going to vote on a given issue, but what the general orientation is, what the tilt of the continent is, how the world feels, you're not going to measure that by asking questions, because nobody has the brains to ask the kind of question which will elicit the kind of answer you need.

Van Doren

                Obviously you couldn't know about the temper of America that way. It isn't mathematical. It isn't statistical. You can't poll it. And certainly, above all, it can't be sampled. No, the question how one finds that out fascinates me too. I'm reminded of certain foreign observers who have been here in the past. De Tocqueville was one of them.

MacLeish

De Tocqueville somehow or other seems to have made some sort of electrical connection, doesn't he?

Van Doren

Yes.

MacLeish

History seems to indicate he did.

Van Doren

People keep on reading his books and finding out what they wouldn't know for themselves. Of course, there were other travelers, sometimes friendly, sometimes hostile: Dickens, Mrs. Trollope, and others.

And then you remember later in the nineteenth century, there was James Bryce who came as an outsider, as an Englishman, a very sober, responsible old English liberal. He looked at the American scene and decided such things as are implied by the title of one of his chapters in *The American Commonwealth*—"Why Great Men Are Never Elected President." What an appalling idea! It really makes your blood run cold, doesn't it? Well, maybe sometimes an observer from the other side is in a better position to see what we can't see for ourselves.

MacLeish

Certainly they're in a better position to observe the American scene than the people inside the country who estimate temper by mathematical means. But, you know, Mark, I believe there are those who have been able to know the true temper of the country. Two examples have occurred to me: looking back with a hundred years' perspective, it now appears that Lincoln, whose adult life had been spent on the frontier, and who was regarded by everyone who knew him as a rather unsophisticated, uncouth man . . .

Van Doren

A country lawyer.

MacLeish

. . . a country lawyer, had a better sense of the temper of the United States, not only North, but North and South, than any man of his time. And a nearer example that I would offer you, not knowing whether you would agree or not, is Sandburg in *The People, Yes*. At a time of great doubt and skepticism in the country, Sandburg somehow had a sense of an optimistic temper, a temper of belief and assertion which later demonstrated itself.

VAN DOREN

Of course, Carl Sandburg is particularly convincing because, among other things, he is humorous. You see, humor is an essential part of it, just as for Lincoln it was an essential part of it.

MACLEISH

It's a unique aspect of the American temper. Anybody who takes the Americans too seriously certainly can't catch their temper, which is why the Marxists were always wrong.

VAN DOREN

They were always wrong. You know, Carl Sandburg, in *The People, Yes,* as I remember that fascinating book, was not doing much more than just writing down what Americans say, what people say, things of a proverbial quality. I've always remembered one thing he wrote down: "He took so much medicine, he was sick for a long time after he got well." (*MacLeish laughs.*) Do you remember that one?

MACLEISH

Yes, or . . . those people in Texas who lived with two strands of barbed wire between them and the North Pole. (*They laugh.*)

VAN DOREN

Or the stranger in an American town who says to the boy: "Boy, where's the post office?" And

215

the boy says, "I don't know." "Well, you don't know much, do you?" "No, but I ain't lost."

MACLEISH (*laughing*)
Yes, yes.

VAN DOREN

Well, that sort of thing is very important. You know what suddenly occurs to me is this: that maybe the temper of a country emerges, transpires, and becomes visible and tangible when some one person speaks.

Now, take Carl Sandburg himself. You read his book, and you realize that although he's doing nothing but quoting other Americans, somehow or other he has composed that work. And there can be an infectious quality in Sandburg which makes a great many people decide, not necessarily to become like him if they aren't already, but makes them say, "Well, I'm already that way, but I want to be even more that way."

MACLEISH

Yes, yes. They're drawn to the temper. Take Robert Frost. Frost, in that sense, has never tested the temper of America, but still, out of the generality of Frost's poems, there comes a sort of a portrait of an American. And it's a portrait that is very infectious. People rather do want to be like that.

216

VAN DOREN

Oh yes. And here's another case that you've already mentioned. How can we determine to what extent Lincoln found out what people were like by observing them? and heaven knows he did. He liked to go among them.

You know, one of the theories about him was that he became the great politician that he became because of the incompatibility between him and his wife. He couldn't stay home. So he had to be out in the corner groceries, he had to be out on the streets talking to men. The same thing is said to be true of Socrates; the reason he became the first-rate philosopher he was was that Xanthippe was a shrew.

MACLEISH

You're not arguing for an unhappy marriage as the basis of political wisdom?

VAN DOREN

I wonder if I am. (*MacLeish laughs.*)

At any rate, take Lincoln; is he just reporting, or is he, out of his own nature, speaking in such a way that other Americans then said, and still may say, "Of course, that's true"?

MACLEISH

Well, that's a good question. It's a very good question.

VAN DOREN

"I'm like that, I guess, and I would like to be still more like that. That's the direction in which I might move." Who can exaggerate the importance of a single person?

MACLEISH

If you put these two men together, you get the possibility of a sort of nexus of observation which is essentially—if you'll forgive me for coming back to our common center of interest—poetic.

It's the poetic thing in Lincoln that makes Lincoln the great observer. It certainly is the poetic thing in Sandburg, this thing that keeps buzzing at him, in addition to everything else that he is, that gives him this quality of feeling.

VAN DOREN

But it was *in* him.

MACLEISH

It was in him, yes.

VAN DOREN

It was *in* him from the first. I don't see why you should doubt that. It was in him from the first. It's his own nature speaking, and finally, his own voice delivering this character. I would settle for that being poetry. I'm sure it is.

MacLeish

Well, assuming all the necessary humilities in the
way of coming to any sort of conclusion, and
agreeing on the impossibility of doing it mathe-
matically, or saying the American people are
moving this way or that way because 745 people
out of a sample of 1,230 say *no* to this and *yes*
to that—excepting all that, have you a sort of
sense of what the temper of the country is now,
in terms of its confidence in itself, which is, I
think, the essential question?

Van Doren

Well, I wonder to what extent those are right
who say that too many of us are afraid to speak
our minds. I'm sure that the most important
American tradition is the tradition of the individual speaking his mind, regardless of how many
people he thinks may disagree with him, and
regardless of any danger in which he may put his
reputation.

I think we've always honored those who, as we
say, spoke out. It might seem to be an unpopular
thing to speak out. It often turns out to have been
a popular thing. Because eventually, the American people do not respect a politician who never
says anything. They want him to say something,
even though they're going to disagree with it.
They'd rather he'd say it—say something—than
say nothing.

Yes, I agree, and though I'm not debating this with you, I really would like to know, I'd like to know in myself—and I don't really know—is it a fear of talking out, or something else?

Take the present wave that many observers have observed, the wave of childish criticism of the President of the United States on the part of American business. Or put it the other way around if you want. But I'm concerned here, primarily, with the attitude toward the President.

Now, certainly there's no basic fear of talking out against the President. People have long said idiotic and ridiculous things without any fear or apprehension, but have they really *said* anything? Have they been expressing more than a temporary irritation or a personal disappointment in relation to a given situation? Are they really expressing a view on the basis of which you could say: "This is what America is like"? I myself doubt it very much. Because a considerable number of American businessmen have a certain attitude toward Kennedy at the present time, I doubt that it means that the American community is pro-business or anti-government. These are more or less expressions of a temporary irritation or, perhaps, even a permanent irritation. But they're personal expressions, and they are not wise; they are childish.

So what you are left with is to wonder how far and how deeply men are really thinking and speaking out boldly on their country's situation? It seems to me, when you are talking about the temper of a country, you must say something about the orientation of the country in relation to its own destiny, what it thinks it is, and what it thinks it's going to become. Perhaps my example is a bad example.

VAN DOREN

No, it's a very interesting example, I would say.

MACLEISH

You see, Mark, it seems to me, when you're talking about the temper of a country, how deeply it believes in itself and in its own destiny, the irritations are not important. I think certain people miss the whole point when they say, I no longer believe in the American destiny, because I think such and such things are going on in Washington; and there are such and such trends in the Congress; and legislation is moving this way and moving that way. This, incidentally, is the kind of mind which says "they," the mysterious "they" with quotation marks around it. "They" are against it. "They" are going to do this or that. This means, in a sense, that "you" don't really believe much in "us" any more. "You" are more concerned about "they" than "you" are about "us."

VAN DOREN

A very good point.

MACLEISH

You may recall at the beginning of this century
the American business community wasn't so
much concerned about "they." Now you may
argue that "they," at that point, hadn't yet begun
to throw "their" weight around. But still the
American business community, America as a business operation, was much more concerned at that
time with what *it* was going to do. And maybe
if one were going to generalize about the temper
of the country today, one would have to say that
these very protestations, these very complaints,
testify to a certain lack of confidence, not in the
country, but in business.

VAN DOREN

What you're really saying is that you think more
persons or more groups of persons should make a
conscious effort to address themselves to the question of what the common good is, what the good
for us all might be, if it ever existed.

MACLEISH

I think what I'm after, Mark, is within what we
were talking about earlier; that insofar as America
is something new, it is an idea; that this idea is
an idea which had its essential expression in the
Declaration of Independence, which had a re-
expression in Lincoln's speech in Philadelphia on

his way to his inauguration, which has had re-expression in generation after generation since. It's an idea which is relatively easy to state, but can only be stated in the greatest language, as in the Declaration.

It is an idea which affirms the supreme worth of the human individual and, through an act of faith, believes in him, and believes that, given the opportunity, he will make for himself a good life.

Now, if this is what America is, if America is that idea, the only real question that anybody ought to be talking about when they talk about the temper of this country is the question of whether or not we're still committed to that idea. I don't think the whining, the complaining, the fearsome talk on the public side, or perhaps the bullying on the government side, really goes to the heart of that question.

It would take another Lincoln to know what our temper is in that regard, and I don't think there's another Lincoln on the political scene now.

VAN DOREN

Well, there's one long perspective to take upon this: the doctrine of equality has what as its source? I would say it has religion as its source, it has the Bible as its source. I believe there's no other book which so completely states, and which so completely justifies, the doctrine of equality,

223

where all men are equal because they're all sons of the same father. I think the Bible is the only thing that makes sense: "Love thy neighbor as thyself," as the Old Testament keeps on saying over and over and over again.

All persons were to have sanctity because they were persons. Then the talk was not so much about the *dignity* of the individual—that's a fairly gray phrase for me—but the *sanctity of the person*. You see, that gives the idea of equality greater depth, I should say. I don't know whether this is true, but you know, Archie, someone has said that democracy has never existed in any place where the Bible didn't exist.

MACLEISH

But is this an historical accident, the fact that democracy developed in the West . . .

VAN DOREN

Yes, it could be.

MACLEISH

Or is it the other way around?

VAN DOREN

I don't know.

MACLEISH

Well, I certainly agree with you that it's only within the frame of the world as seen through the window of the Bible that it's possible to conceive of a man, any man, as having the kind of importance that in the founding of this country it was assumed that he had.

VAN DOREN

Yes, and I think we must still somehow or other continue to be able to assume that every man has this kind of importance. If not, we're lost. I think what you and I are saying today we should say at the tops of our voices.

MACLEISH

Yes, certainly at the tops of our voices, but still, Mark, if one is inquiring about the temper of one's country one is bound to ask whether there is *evidence* that the country has made the supreme commitment to the sanctity of every person that it ought to have made.

VAN DOREN

The fact that it's difficult to see the signs doesn't necessarily mean that they don't exist. The signs are there to be seen, if we could understand them. It's difficult because the face of the country changes every minute, and young people, in particular, are being asked to consider a different transformation every year of their lives.

MACLEISH

Maybe this accounts for some of the rather cynical, snotty young reactionaries who tear down

225

these beliefs, who make liberalism a fabricated enemy for themselves, regarding as liberals all men who really believe in the concept we're talking about. This kind of young man is a man who is really fearful at heart. He's also a man with an extraordinary poverty of spiritual power.

VAN DOREN

I don't need to remind you, Archie, that this reached a critical stage not long ago when word came to us of the brainwashing of American prisoners in Korea. It appeared then, at least so it was said, that some of our men in Korea who were put under a strain, and under that strain were asked to remember what this country was about, and what they were there for, couldn't do it.

MACLEISH

One wonders, Mark, whether this incapacity was the result of brainwashing, or whether it was the result of the fact that very little grafting into a man of the fundamental tree of human liberty took place in their childhood.

VAN DOREN

That's right; that's what was said by many people. These boys had not somehow or other ever been told, nor had they ever defined from their own observation, what the American experience was all about.

MacLeish

I've seen criticisms of the curricula of the American high schools, which indicate that because individual civil liberties, fundamental American concepts, are now controversial in certain areas where McCarthyism left its hairy touch, or where the John Birch Society is now leaving its rather dirty bird tracks, that the basic American concept is barely touched on, is passed over lightly, or is taught by uninspired teachers who themselves don't understand what they're talking about. Whether this sort of criticism is justified I don't know. I've never made such an examination myself, but I'll bet you anything it is.

Van Doren

You mean that the criticism is valid?

MacLeish

I think the criticisms are valid, that only in the best high schools do the teachers really deal at all with the fundamental American concept.

Van Doren

Well, maybe everyone should begin self-examination at home. Do you and I have this faith to the limit? If the answer is yes, and I think it is, if we have this faith to the limit, that's all we can do, plus say so. We should say so whenever we can, and wherever we can.

You see, Archie, I don't think it's a question of

what other people think; more importantly it's
what *we* think. And maybe that's what saves the
society; every member in it looking within himself and saying, "Who am I? What do *I* think?"
Not, "What does my neighbor think?" If he believes in what *he* thinks, and says so, his neighbor is probably changed.

MacLeish

And yet in the American conception of the place
of man in the universe, the person that one values
isn't oneself. The person that one values most is
those other selves with which one has to do in
one's life. Isn't that so?

Van Doren

Yes, but I think we can have faith in others,
which I think we must have, only when we have
faith in ourselves, when we have no doubt about
ourselves. You see, maybe this incessant search,
this burrowing and buzzing into the beliefs of
others comes from a lack of conviction in our beliefs; we don't know what we think, so we don't
want to know what anyone thinks.

MacLeish

I thought you were going to say the opposite.
Maybe one of the results of burrowing into the
depths and interstices of the self—which comes
out of the development of Freudian psychology
—is an increasing doubt as to the integrity and
wholeness of other human beings.

VAN DOREN

Put it this way, Archie. You know the famous paradox, that whenever you have written an entirely personal poem or piece of prose, whenever you have really delivered the goods so far as you yourself are concerned, and said what you thought, what happened? You found that everybody else understood you, didn't you?

MACLEISH

I wish I could say yes to that; at least, I hope so.

VAN DOREN

It's been my experience. Whenever I have been afraid that my work was so personal that no one could understand it, everybody did understand it. When I tried to speak for others, they didn't know what I was talking about.

MACLEISH

That's very wise. That's wise and well said, and I really think it's true. But I don't draw the same conclusion from this very wise saying of yours that you do. I don't think that one can search one's own heart to find if one holds the conviction which is fundamental to this Republic. I don't find that it is in the searching of oneself that that realization comes.

I think the realization comes when you arrive at a point in your life—which some men do earlier, some later, and some not at all—a point

229

at which you cannot look into any other human face without seeing there everything that you value in yourself. You see something there that you respect as much as you could possibly respect yourself, something that can't be hurt, can't be limited, and can't be obstructed.

VAN DOREN

Well, now I'm going to be stubborn about this, only because you are. For instance, what is courtesy? Courtesy consists in assuming that everyone else is a gentleman, not in wondering whether he is or not, but in just assuming that he is. To be a gentleman is to be nothing, I say, except a man who thinks all other men are gentlemen.

Now, it may seem naïve sometimes to make this assumption, but it's astonishing how many gentlemen you create by making such an assumption, and how many ladies you can create by assuming that all women are ladies.

Lincoln made us all political philosophers by being a political philosopher in our presence. He paid us the supreme compliment of believing we could understand him, and you know he said very closely reasoned things. It took lots of attention, and we gave it to him.

MACLEISH

Perhaps the essence of agreement, for me, is to

say that I think you have demonstrated exactly
what I am trying to say.

VAN DOREN

Yes. I don't think we're really disagreeing.

MACLEISH

It does seem to me that we agree, except that I
am taking two steps, two bites of the cherry.

VAN DOREN

Maybe I'm missing a step here.

MACLEISH

Well, the first bite of this cherry—the essential
thing—is to realize what you are as a "person."
This you can learn only in yourself. You learn it
in yourself in relation to others. You learn it in
relation to your mother, your father, your brothers, your sisters, your friends. But you learn it *in*
yourself, and sooner or later, if the process of your
education proceeds far enough so that you become mature, you realize that you are a person,
for better or for worse, with all your faults upon
you, and that you have a kind of value which is
not limited by the fact that you're going to die.
You're a mortal, but you're valuable nevertheless.
That, I think, is the first bite in the cherry. You
have to feel what a human being is, know what a
human being is.

231

The second bite of the cherry, and the really important one so far as the political organization goes, is the realization that if you are a "person," then so is he and he, and he and he.

VAN DOREN

That's right. I think that is an act of faith too. I think that is something you must be able to believe, because it's true. I pity those who can't believe it, who despise others because they're not the same as themselves.

You see, what turns out to be true, I think, is this: although we're all different from one another so that no one of us is mistaken for another, yet the resemblances among us are probably more important than the differences.

You know, we are the same in many, many respects. The fact that you and I are talking, using the English language with each other, implies that we think we have the same mind.

MACLEISH

Well, the miraculous thing is that it's possible for two human beings to talk with each other in words about what to them is simply impressions or depths of feeling so that somehow or other agreement does become possible.

VAN DOREN

But the third thing out there, what we're really

talking about, is more important than either one of us.

MACLEISH

Yes, that's true. I think the reason why America is of such tremendous and fundamental importance to you and me is not that you or I are patrioteers who feel we're only dressed when we have a flag wrapped around us; the reason it's so important is that America *is* that third thing out there.

America is a concept of what life could be like if you had an understanding of the human self in yourself, a respect for the human self in others, and a political mechanism which would make it work. And the word *freedom*, I think, is a word which simply describes the viability of this kind of relationship. It describes a man not free simply of government supervision, of policemen, of bullying Southern cops, of any of the other tyrants who gag the world. It means that a man is free of the constant attrition of other people's suspicion and denigration, and this achieved is what America is. And from that point of view, America is something worth any man's belief and any man's passionate loyalty!

VAN DOREN

Of course it is. You know, Archie, I'm suddenly reminded of Socrates' famous injunction, "Know

233

thyself." Everything that we don't owe to the Jews, we owe to the Greeks. Everything that we don't owe to the Greeks, we owe to the Jews. At least, I suspect that's the case. But certainly we owe Socrates those two words, which in my opinion are often misunderstood to mean "know thyself" as an end in itself, as if that were anything to know.

I believe he meant know yourself, know the mind or the spirit that's in you, because that's what's in all men. I think he meant, for instance: Do not consider what you happen to think about something; consider what could be thought about something by you if you used your mind well.

MACLEISH

In other words, know the world, know the possibilities of the world.

VAN DOREN

That's right.

MACLEISH

Know yourself, because that's where you'll find it.

VAN DOREN

That's where you'll find it. You'll find that all men are alike finally. Through the mere fact that they discourse, they will be asserting a faith in the possibilities of discourse.

MacLeish

To know thyself means . . .

Van Doren

To know the man that is in you.

MacLeish

And that man is also the descendant of other men.

Van Doren

He's *all* men . . .

MacLeish

And the descendant of other particular men.

Van Doren

Yes.

MacLeish

Of what particular man are you the product, Mark? Your name is obviously Dutch, isn't it?

Van Doren *(laughs)*

Yes, it's Dutch, but I never feel like a Dutchman.

MacLeish

How do you know how a Dutchman feels?

Van Doren

"Know thyself." I never say to myself I am Dutch, and . . .

235

MacLeish

How far back did you have Dutch antecedents?

Van Doren

Well, the Dutchman who started our family in this country came to this country in 1699. And all of the people who have my name seem to come from him. All of the records taper back to this one man, Pieter Van Doorn, who landed on the shores of New Jersey, in Monmouth County, in 1699.

MacLeish

How'd he move west, he and his descendants?

Van Doren

Well, gradually, as always happened.

MacLeish

Through Pennsylvania?

Van Doren

Up through Pennsylvania, northern New Jersey, then into Pennsylvania; then into New York State, and then when the Erie Canal was opened they went west into northern Illinois.

I lived in the part of Illinois where two waves of immigration had met; the wave from the South, from Kentucky and Virginia, and the wave from the North and the East. We had people around us who were originally Southern, but the people we knew best, the people we felt most at home with, were the Northerners—as we'd call them—who had come from New York State, Pennsylvania, New England, and whatnot. I'm always glad that I knew both kinds of people. They were very different.

MACLEISH

Where did your mothers come from? All your mothers, and mothers, and mothers?

VAN DOREN

My mother's father was German. His name was Butz, and curiously enough he came from New Jersey also. Eventually he moved to Pennsylvania, and then to Ohio. He was a part of the same movement, the same immigration west. What about your beginnings?

MACLEISH

Well, mine is a simple story. My mother's family's name was Hillard.

VAN DOREN

Hillard?

MACLEISH

H-i-l-l-a-r-d, without an extra "i." Her father was a Congregational minister in Connecticut. His antecedents were sea captains, mostly out of the small ports along the New England coast in the North Atlantic trade, starting with Captain

237

Moses Hillard, and on back through. Further back there were the Brewsters: Elder Brewster, of course, was the minister of the *Mayflower*. So you see, my mother's family is straight Connecticut Yankee.

My father was a Scotsman, born in Glasgow, the son of a small, impoverished shopkeeper. He was born, incidentally, much too early to be my father. That sounds like James Joyce's remark to Yeats, "You were born too early to be influenced by me." Well, in any event, my father was born too early to be my father. He was born in the year of Queen Victoria's Coronation in '38. He ran away from home and went to London.

VAN DOREN

Your father was born in 1838?

MACLEISH

In '38.

VAN DOREN

That's remarkable.

MACLEISH

It is remarkable. He lived the life of a small shop-keeper much like Dickens describes in his Scrooge story. He came to the United States when he was eighteen years old. And went to a place he'd heard of called Chicago, which was out in your state of

Illinois, where you Van Dorens were then established. Or were you there then?

VAN DOREN

Oh, yes, about that time. My father was born there in '57.

MACLEISH

My father got there in '56.

VAN DOREN

Amazing!

MACLEISH

And so eventually his third wife—his first two having died—became my mother. And there you have the combination of a Scottish Calvinistic conscience and a Yankee Calvinistic conscience, and the net result of that is me.

VAN DOREN

But, Archie, you say your father was born in '38.

MACLEISH

That's right.

VAN DOREN

Well, he must have been by no means a young man when you were born.

MACLEISH

Oh, he was over fifty when I was born.

VAN DOREN

I see. Because my *grand*father, my mother's father, was born in '35. So you see what was troubling me for a minute. By the way, my paternal grandmother was English. She came from Lancashire.

MacLEISH

Are you quite sure you have no Scots blood?

VAN DOREN

No, I'm afraid not. I wish I did.

MacLEISH

I wish you did too.

VAN DOREN

There may be a little bit in there, but I never heard of it.

MacLEISH

Mark, in this reminiscent vein, I was going to ask, has it ever occurred to you that the generation to which you and I belong is certainly, in one way, the most remarkable generation that has ever existed anywhere. You and I were born and grew up as little boys in a world in which you went to church back of a pair of horses, a world in which there was no communication except by neighbors coming in, or you going out . . .

Van Doren

Or letters.

MacLeish

Or letters, and they were slow enough. A world of a very modest and moderate standard of living, except for certain very rich men who were reprehended by all and sundry. We lived through that period, and now in continuing vitality we find ourselves in a world in which not one of the basic circumscribing circumstances of our lives as children exists any longer.

Van Doren

True.

MacLeish

Today, we move in a different way, communicate in a different way, live at a different level, eat different foods, and you know, perhaps aren't really very much happier when you come down to it.

Van Doren

I often wonder how different we are, if at all, because of all these changes in our physical environment. We have all these things that work for us; we have these things that move us about rapidly, so that we're always on the move, we're always going somewhere, even when we don't want to.

We're restless, I suppose. All people are these days. But I wonder to what extent we're different.

You know, one thing you said interested me; you spoke of communications. My brother Carl, who is nine years older than I, remembers that in our little town down there in Illinois, in Hope, Illinois . . .

MacLeish

Was that the name of your town before you moved to Urbana?

Van Doren

Yes, there had been three little towns.

MacLeish

Not Faith and Charity?

Van Doren

Faith, Hope, and Charity.

MacLeish

Really?

Van Doren

My grandfather named them. My mother's father. Faith, Hope, and Charity. Now only Hope survives; the others are not there at all. Hope has a population of thirty-four.

MacLeish

Wasn't Charity, in St. Paul's mind, the greatest of these three?

Van Doren

Yes, that's true, but Charity "ain't there no more." Still, people talk about Charity as a community. They say, "Oh, he comes from out near Charity." But there's no town there any more.

Well, in any event, when I was born in '94, my brother Carl was nine years old, and, of course, he remembered everybody in our community; the farmers, my father, who was a doctor, and simply everybody. And he told me how everybody would go down with a great eagerness to the country store once a month to get copies of the *Strand* magazine, the English magazine, the *Strand*. Do you know why?

MacLeish

No.

Van Doren

Because every month the *Strand* contained a story about Sherlock Holmes.

MacLeish

Well, I'll be shot!

Van Doren

Who was, you know, and is, probably the most

completely successful character in modern fiction.

MacLeish

And everybody in Central Illinois was following Sherlock Holmes?

Van Doren

The farmers thought of nothing else. They wanted to know what his next adventure was going to be. The *Strand* magazine had a circulation that was unlimited in the English-speaking world. It even reached the little place of Hope, Illinois.

MacLeish

And largely due to Sherlock Holmes.

Van Doren

Oh, entirely, yes. The stories of Conan Doyle were appearing, and these people read about London and Baker Street, and the railways, and the express trains that went down to Essex and got Sherlock Holmes there just in time to apprehend the murderer.

MacLeish

Yes, yes, yes.

Van Doren

They read that as if it were home ground for them. What I'm really saying is that what happened back there isn't too different from what can happen now when we follow serials on television with the same eagerness.

MacLeish

Well, except that then it happened with a greater delay, with more anticipation, and the substance when you got to it was perhaps a little better.

Van Doren

There was a lot of substance. And you know, Archie, I'm not joking when I say that Sherlock Holmes may be the one character in modern fiction who is still universally known. He was completely created, whatever his limitations. He's just as clear as if he were etched. Almost everybody knows what he looked like with his pipe and cap, and they know a few things that he did.

MacLeish

It's interesting to contrast that with *War and Peace*. It's admired as the greatest novel ever written, but not everybody can name all the . . .

Van Doren

. . . people in it.

MacLeish

Another thing I'm curious about, Mark, is the differences, if any, between our generation when we were youngsters, and the young generations of

245

today. For forty years you taught a number of generations of youngsters coming along. Inevitably, you must have contrasted them in your mind with the youngster you yourself were and the people who grew up around you. You must have come to some conclusions on a subject which disturbs so many people: the question of whether the youth of America are going to hell in a hack or in a buggy?

Certainly you must have had many, many friends among your students, whom you knew not simply as students, but who have been continuing friendships in your life. In fact, I know this is true, because I suppose no teacher ever had more student friends than you.

VAN DOREN

Well, I did and I'm very proud of the fact that I have friends who once were students, but I should say this: I never expressly made an attempt to cultivate students as friends. I said this in public once, and I was misunderstood for saying it, probably because I didn't say it right. But I wanted to have my students as students first of all. If they wanted me to be their friend they had to make the move. And plenty of them did, and I was happy that they did. A number of them from the very beginning are still close friends of mine. I could name many of them, but I don't know that I want to do that because, in one sense, all of them were friends. You know, people who consider the same subject together become friends by virtue of that mere fact.

MacLeish

If they really consider it together.

Van Doren

And do not consider themselves.

MacLeish

Yes.

Van Doren

I consider a good situation in teaching to be one in which neither the teacher nor the student is as important as the subject. There it is, the subject is the third thing out there; that's what they're both contemplating. That brings them together, that makes them equal in a very curious sense. It makes them one.

MacLeish

Mark, going down through the academic generations of your forty-odd years of teaching, do you see a graph that rises, a graph that falls, or a graph that just doesn't do much but wobble up and down?

Van Doren

I'm afraid that last is true. I'm always disappointing people who ask me what the difference is.

MacLeish

What *do* you think about American youth?

Van Doren

What I always say is I don't see any difference. To me students tend to be students always. And they've been more alike than they were different.

I grant there were minor differences from time to time. During World War II there were not many students, because most of them were away. Immediately after the war there were the GI students, somewhat older than the others, and they were mixed up with the young ones. During the Depression years, the serious Depression years, there were students interested in society in a very special way. I remember one of them one time came to me and said, "I suggest that you join a certain committee." You know we were all joining committees then, or being asked to. And I said, "What is it?" He defined it for me and it sounded good to me, so I joined it. A few weeks later he came to me again and said, "Do you remember that committee that I asked you to join?" I said, "Yes." He said, "Now I suggest that you resign, because it's a Communist committee."

Well, that sort of thing went on then, but I think those are minor differences. I hold on rather stubbornly to the notion that students are very much alike at all times. When I go now to other universities and colleges and meet students at re-

ceptions after my appearances, it occurs to me
that they're just the same as students everywhere.
Perhaps I shouldn't say this, but to me there's
nothing special about them. Do you have that
feeling?

MacLeish

Well, how do you explain my conviction, based
on very much less teaching than yours . . .

Van Doren

But fifteen years isn't . . .

MacLeish

. . . a mere twelve years, and late in my life,
you know.

Van Doren

I see.

MacLeish

How do you explain my conviction that the students that I taught at Harvard, the students there
in the fifties were so much better, man for man,
group for group, class for class, than my con-
temporaries at Yale and the Harvard Law School?
The students of the fifties were so much better,
or seemed to me so much better, not only in terms
of the readiness of their intelligences but really in
their qualities as human beings. They seemed to
be more sensitive, more sensible, more adult. Is

this a pure delusion? Or was it simply that I had forgotten what the young were like?

VAN DOREN

Well, it's a delusion I love you for, Archie. I don't think they were as much better as you thought. But you thought well of them, which you should have. I think any teacher should think highly of his students, and should have illusions about them, if you please. Those illusions are often shattered when you read an examination paper (*MacLeish laughs*), but I don't think that's very important. After all, they're not writers, you know.

MACLEISH

Yes.

VAN DOREN

And yet even though they write poor examinations, you can have faith that they understand a great deal more than they are able to say.

MACLEISH

You didn't have girls in your classes, did you?

VAN DOREN

No, I never did. Oh, a few got in there from Barnard College and elsewhere.

MACLEISH

Well, one of the things at Harvard which I hadn't

been prepared for when I went there to teach was the existence of the Radcliffe girl. She represented about 30 percent of the students enrolled in the courses I was teaching.

VAN DOREN

There are that many, are there?

MACLEISH

Yes, and I found that the Radcliffe girl leavened the lump. She leavened it in such a way that I'd go out of a lecture thinking, "My goodness, I really touched them," when all I probably meant was that three girls looked back at me with alive faces as though they saw what I was driving at. Maybe they didn't, I don't know.

VAN DOREN

Well, I think you have to be a sucker and believe that they did. (*MacLeish laughs.*) After all, it comes down to individuals, it comes down to this: in any given generation of college students there can be a single student who probably would have been just what he was at any time, in any generation. For example, in the late thirties Thomas Merton was a student of mine. You must know his name.

MACLEISH

Yes, I know who he is.

251

VAN DOREN

Today he is incomparably brilliant and lovely, and charming.

MACLEISH

Was he brilliant as an undergraduate?

VAN DOREN

Oh yes.

MACLEISH

Was it clear at that time that he had a vocation?

VAN DOREN

None whatever, no. That happened after he left college, shortly after. As an undergraduate he was a poet, and he was an editor of the college humorous magazine. He was a very witty man, and still is. I go to see him in his monastery once in a while. I've been there three or four times.

MACLEISH

Where is his monastery?

VAN DOREN

At a place called Trappist, Kentucky. I mean that's the post office. You know, as a Trappist monk, Merton is committed to a vow of silence, but he's a great talker, and when I go down there he always gets a dispensation and we walk around and talk our heads off all day long. He gets in the

car and we drive and see a tobacco barn or this
or that and have a grand time.

MacLeish

How can a great talker take a vow of silence without suffering agonies?

Van Doren

I've often wondered. I've often wondered. But
I'm sure he would have been the same anywhere,
any time. And I think that would be true of
Lionel Trilling. He's the same man now that he
was when he was a student of mine.

You know, people don't change too much. I remember Trilling distinctly. I wrote about him.
He was one of several Jewish students that had
particularly impressed me in the twenties. I remember the editor of the *Menorah Journal* heard
that I admired some of my Jewish students, and
asked me if I wouldn't write an article about
them. Well, I did. One of these students was
Lionel Trilling. Another was Louis Zukofsky. I
don't know whether you know Zukofsky's poetry
or not?

MacLeish

No, I don't know him.

Van Doren

He was a protégé of Ezra Pound and William

Carlos Williams. Still another was Clifton Fadiman, and there were others. Well, I wrote an article for the *Menorah* and said I couldn't write about these Jewish students as Jews, because each one was different from the others. I wasn't able to locate any quality in them merely because they were Jews, but it happened that as individuals they had all impressed me. Each one of them was what he was. Trilling was not like any of the others, and, of course, he wasn't like Thomas Merton. He wasn't like anyone of hundreds that I could name.

Maybe I'm just being stubborn about this, but I refuse to generalize about the generations of students.

MacLeish

Oh, I'm sure you're right. After all, why should human nature change in a period of forty years?

Van Doren

I don't think it does or can.

MacLeish

I do think the quality of instruction is probably one of the things that has changed. My period at Yale was a period which had some very great teachers: Chauncey Tinker and others. But it was also the blue-sweater era. The fact that I played football at Yale was much more important to me than the fact that I attended courses in this, that, and the other. And this was the general view of the college, but I think that sort of thing has changed.

The intellectual life, if you can give that dreadful title to something which is much more important than that, has become an accepted way of life. To-day, scholastic or intellectual success is the most important thing in the world to a youngster in any good American college, whereas forty years ago, fifty years ago, it wasn't.

But that's enough of this. I'm famished. Let's go inside where it's cooler, Mark. Nellie should have converted those groceries into a lovely lunch by this time.

VAN DOREN

Yes, that's a good idea. We've worked up quite an appetite.

MacLeish and Van Doren enter the house for lunch. Then, as is their custom, they retire to the coolness of the music room-study.

VAN DOREN

Archie, after your undergraduate days at Yale, I know you went on and studied law at Harvard. I've always marveled at that, and have been some-what curious . . .

255

MacLeish

Well, I went to the Harvard Law School because I wanted to marry Ada. I wanted to marry her fast, and I had the feeling, which turned out to be justified, that my father, who was a Scotsman, who admired scholarship, would probably support me for a while longer if I went to some scholarly institution. So I went to the Harvard Law School.

Van Doren

You mean a professional institution, perhaps?

MacLeish

Professional institution, yes. So I went to the Harvard Law School. The war intervened and I was away for two years, but I came back.

You know, Mark, I feel very clearly in my own mind that the most important thing that ever happened to me in terms of formal education happened at the Harvard Law School, a school which had nothing to do with my paramount interests, because even then I had only one passion, and that was to try to write verse.

Van Doren

That's why I was curious.

MacLeish

Somehow or other, Mark, instruction in the law, particularly instruction in the law given at the level of the Harvard Law School, which is a very high level, and given in the Socratic method— which was then the only method of instruction— conveys a sense that an undergraduate education doesn't convey. Learning the law there provided a sense of the tradition of human conduct, action, knowledge, values, morality, and so forth. The glacier slowly moves, and you felt yourself part of the glacier. For the first time you were drawn into something.

VAN DOREN

Yes.

MACLEISH

You're not, as in the study of literature, an observer on the outside saying, "Well, that's the way *he* wrote, and that's the way *he* wrote, and I like *him,* and I don't like *him.*" You're drawn in because you have to be drawn in. And this seems to me to be a vitally important part of an education that is not only usable, but instructive in the most profound sense, instructive in the sense of where you are in society, and what society is to you.

VAN DOREN

Oh, yes. I'm sure of that. You remember Whitehead, the philosopher, once said, "Education is finally specialist." In other words, one is not educated altogether until one has narrowed his ac-

257

tivity to a particular field of study where he tries to meet a standard of proficiency which all other must meet.

I know students graduating from Columbia College used to come to me with rather sad faces and say, "Well, now I have to stop being a real student, and study only law or only medicine." And I said: "Well, don't you realize it's just beginning for you? You're not going to narrow yourself because you go through a narrow door."

MacLeish

It's like saying, "I have to live only life."

Van Doren

That's right, that's wonderful. I said, "Once you get through this narrow door, you've got the whole world there." I said, "Nobody ever felt sorry for Shakespeare because he was nothing but a poet. Nobody ever felt sorry for Rembrandt because he was nothing but a painter. You have to be something."

MacLeish

It's really a question of a man's ultimate beliefs, the beliefs that form him, the beliefs to which he will cling in spite of everything, in spite of certain narrow doors.

For example, Learned Hand was a lawyer who was an agnostic, who was profoundly skeptical about answers, not only easy answers, but any answers. But Learned Hand was a man who, by virtue of his life as a lawyer, and his long life as a judge, had found himself anchors in which not only I, but anyone, could believe.

VAN DOREN

Yes.

MACLEISH

They weren't perhaps, from the spiritual point of view, the most exalted, and yet from the human point of view nothing was more exalted.

VAN DOREN

Particularly his conception of liberty, as I understand it.

MACLEISH

And his conception of the role of man. Did I ever tell you the story of how I went up to see "B" Hand at his chambers in New York and asked him if he would read the Voice of God in *JB*? You know, at the end of *JB* there's this long passage in which the distant Voice, confronting *JB*, begins that great passage: "Where wast thou when I laid the foundations of the universe?"

VAN DOREN

Yes.

MacLeish

Well, we had it read by an actor, and the actor, try as he might, sounded like an actor.

Van Doren (*laughing*)
Yes.

MacLeish

What one needed was a voice. One needed authority, one needed, above all, an old man's voice. So it occurred to me, knowing Learned Hand— "B" Hand—as we called him . . .

Van Doren

Why was he called "B," by the way?

MacLeish

His name was Billings Learned Hand.

Van Doren

Oh, yes, yes, I'd forgotten that.

MacLeish

And all his friends called him "B."

Van Doren

Yes.

MacLeish

Knowing "B" the way I knew him, I thought the thing to do perhaps was to try it out and see if he would, by chance, agree to do it. So I called up his wife and asked if I could come to see him in his chambers, and it was agreed that I could. And I flew up to New York. We were then opening in Washington.

Well, when I entered his chambers, he looked at me very skeptically. He told me afterwards he thought I was coming to ask him to make a speech and he was all ready to say no. I remember I said, " 'B,' I'm going to leave this door open behind me if you don't mind, because I want to be able to get out of here fast." And then I told him what it was I wanted.

He listened to me very attentively, and then he was suddenly convulsed with laughter. He doubled up at his desk, and his face turned scarlet. He couldn't stop laughing. And he finally said, panting between laughs, "Archie, do you know what my relations are up There?" (*MacLeish and Van Doren laugh.*) Here he was invited to read the Voice of God, and he had been denying the existence of God all his life long.

But you know, Mark, his denial of the existence of God was in a very believable way an affirmation of his belief in a human true north.

VAN DOREN

Yes, I know, it can be.

MacLeish

For him there was a true north in human life. He was a very great man, and I think very largely because he was so skeptical.

Van Doren

Well, did he read it? Did he do the reading?

MacLeish

He did it. Oh yes, he did it.

Van Doren

You mean that's what we heard in the play?

MacLeish

No. Alas, no. The voice was exactly right. It was an old man's voice. It was a voice full of authority. It really shook your heart. The trouble was that, in between, when he caught his breath, there was a rasping sound that the engineers couldn't eliminate. And the tape was never used.

Van Doren

Oh dear.

MacLeish

It was terribly sad. I understand "B" was very anxious to have it used.

Van Doren

Yes, of course he was.

262

MacLeish

He was proud of it.

Van Doren

Well then, take Learned Hand: no one ever felt sorry for him because he was nothing but a lawyer. After all, that's how he became the big man he was. We have to be one thing in order to be everything.

It's a curious thing. We can't be all things, jacks of all trades. And you know every discipline—to take a rather stuffy word—every study really embraces everything before it finishes. Think what a person has to know in order to be a truly good doctor, or a good poet, or a good anything.

MacLeish

Take another lawyer, take Felix Frankfurter.

Van Doren

Yes.

MacLeish

He is a man with the most universal interests; there is nothing in the world Felix isn't interested in.

Van Doren

I know that.

MacLeish

And I think it's because of the great circumference of his interests that his work as a lawyer and his work as a judge has been what it is; and above all, that his human quality has been what it is.

This touches upon something else, Mark, that we haven't really talked about. We've only talked around the edges of it. It would be impossible to summarize Felix Frankfurter in any whole or meaningful way, without talking about the fact that he had what one calls, lightly, a genius for friendship. He has more friends than anybody I know, and by more friends I mean people whose lives he is constantly in touch with, people to whom he is always writing those little personal notes he writes up on the bench.

His mind is everywhere with all these people, people in England, people on the Continent, people all over the United States, people of all sorts and kinds and shapes. And there is something of significance in that fact in his life. There is a relationship, I think, between the scope of his human attachment and human concern, and the extraordinary vitality of the man, the amazing vitality of the man. This is the kind of relationship, the kind of friendship that works both ways, doesn't it?

Van Doren

Oh yes.

MacLeish

> This kind of passionate friendship is not giving, and it's not receiving; it's like some sort of dynamo in operation that creates the force by which people live.

Van Doren

> You know, a few weeks ago I saw this happen in my own case with him. I had never met him, but he and I were both to speak at the dinner for Robert Frost's eighty-eighth birthday.

MacLeish

> Which was almost the last thing that happened to him before he became ill, wasn't it?

Van Doren

> Yes, I believe so. We were sat at opposite ends of a long speakers' table, and I looked down the table as we assembled and I saw him there. Of course, I recognized him from the many, many pictures of him I have seen.
>
> And as I sat there I said to myself: "I wonder if I should get up and go and introduce myself to him. I should like to very much, but I'm not sure that it would mean anything to him." At that moment he rose and came down the table. I didn't know where he was going, but he was coming to me.

MACLEISH

Yes, yes.

VAN DOREN

Well, he shook my hand and said: "I'm so glad to know you at last. I've been sitting by your wife and we've been talking. It was quite old-homey."

MACLEISH

And naturally when he sat down beside Dorothy what he had said was, "Where's Mark?"

VAN DOREN

Yes, he did. He had said that. Well, it's a curious thing what you say about him because it suddenly clicks with me that it was perfectly expressed by that one thing he did.

MACLEISH

You know, Mark, it occurs to me that Felix too with all his genius for friendship has his doubts about the Almighty as "B" had—as I daresay you have, Mark. I know for myself if I were put through the orange squeezer and squeezed to the point where the pips began to squeak, I think I too would have to say that I'm not really sure whether I believe in any easily definable conception of God or not. I certainly don't believe in an anthropomorphic god. I don't believe in a god who spends his time thinking about me, and I would find it rather shameful to believe in a god simply because he spent his time thinking about me. I don't mean to say that it's shameful in anybody else, but I would think it was shameful in myself.

I do think if I were squeezed down to the point where the pips began to emit high, shrill sounds, I would have to say, that what I surely do believe in is the unspeakable, infinite, immeasurable, spiritual capacity of that thing called a man; a capacity which expresses itself in so many ways, but expresses itself nowhere more perfectly than in the capacity for friendship, which is really a capacity for love.

VAN DOREN

Yes.

MACLEISH

What I mean by love is not the love that desires something for itself, but the kind of relationship which gives itself in praise and wonder and awe. This is something that is beyond the reach of the imagination to understand, and it is worth believing in.

VAN DOREN

Well, you know, I think we suddenly touch there again upon a theme that we've touched upon many times before: Friendship makes men equal, does it not?

267

MacLeish

There can't be friendship without equality.

Van Doren

No, there cannot be. Friendship makes men equal. Loves makes persons equal. When you love another person, you love him as another person. He's not a projection of you. He's not a copy of you. You love him because he is not you. Isn't that true?

MacLeish

Yes.

Van Doren

I don't believe you love him unless you love him as another person.

MacLeish

And it's for the explicit reason, if you will give me a parenthesis, that it's impossible, really, to love yourself. People talk about loving themselves. This is greed. You can't love yourself. Love involves an opposite. Love only exists in opposites.

Van Doren

And that person whom you love you want to continue to be just what he is. You don't want to change him. You don't criticize him very much, do you? You don't want to rebuild him or recreate him. You want him to be what he is. You accept him.

Well, that acceptance, that willingness to accept, and that delight in acceptance of others, seems to me to be inseparable from the idea of equality, be it political, social, moral, or anything you please.

MacLeish

This love comes, Mark—to repeat what I said a minute ago—it comes very close to being the ultimate of which the human spirit is capable. Wonder and awe sound as though they went beyond it, but they don't go beyond it, because one can't feel either wonder or awe toward anything which one isn't able to sense. And to sense what is wonderful and what is awe-full is, in a sense, to love it too.

Van Doren

You know, I was interested in your remark that it was very difficult for you to conceive of God. It ought to be difficult. I can't either. I'm always impressed by the fact that those who speak most glibly of God probably have less right to than those who find it difficult to.

I remember Maxim Gorky's marvelous little book of reminiscences of Tolstoy. Tolstoy, as an old man, saw a good deal of this younger writer, Maxim Gorky, you know. And Gorky wrote a little volume recording his impressions of Tolstoy. He said he was watching Tolstoy during the time when Tolstoy was trying to become religious.

Tolstoy was trying to accept God, but it was terribly hard for him because he was fighting it all the time. He didn't want to. Gorky said sometimes it was like two bears in one den.

MacLeish

Only one of whom was visible.

Van Doren

Yes. Isn't it a wonderful image?

MacLeish

Yes, that's very good.

Van Doren

What I mean is, I take that sort of religion much more seriously than the religion which is easily worn.

MacLeish

Or, take the other side of it. I don't suppose there is more difficult or obviously painful writing anywhere in Dostoevski—more wonderful writing—than those pages in which Father Zossima attempts to communicate his sense of God. If there ever were words written out of blood and suffering, it was those words.

Van Doren

The whole point was, that it was not easy.

MacLeish

I agree with you so much that the man who can simply say God and think he's said something is really the blasphemer.

Van Doren

Yes. I agree with you. As a matter of fact, it is well to remember the Old Testament here. God's people, His own people, were always denying Him, always forgetting Him, always rejecting Him, and groaning and complaining. You remember how they did?

MacLeish

Yes.

Van Doren

The last thing they were was pious. It was awfully hard for them to remember Him and to believe in Him. I think that's one reason we somehow take their religion seriously. It's one of the reasons. They were backsliding, and He was always angry at them, and yet He always forgave them. It was a constant quarrel.

MacLeish

Yes, the Old Testament is really, considered in its whole scope, a search for God. It begins with God, but it's the account of a search for God.

Van Doren

Well, it begins with God and then it's as if He

had been lost, and they were looking for Him all that time.

MacLeish

All the wrestling with the Angel and all the rest of it.

They come to a stop, each withdrawing into his own thoughts; the room is suddenly sullen with the heat of the lowering afternoon sun.

MacLeish

Mark, it's getting unbearably warm. Are you game for a swim in the upper pond? There's nothing like pond water, on a sultry day.

Van Doren

Well, I'm not much of a swimmer as you know, Archie, but let's go. It might be cooler there. And I can watch you.

MacLeish and Van Doren leave the house, drive down the hill behind the house to the lower pond, and park. They set off on foot along the wood path leading to the upper pond. They arrive, and MacLeish strips and dives flatly into the still pond. Van Doren, on the bank, stands straight among a clump of dipping birches.

MacLeish

It's a lovely temperature, Mark. You're crazy if you don't come in.

VAN DOREN

It looks good.

MACLEISH

I was hoping we'd see some of those wood ducks
here.

VAN DOREN

What does a wood duck look like? I'm not sure.
Is it colored?

MACLEISH

Most beautiful bird in the world. The male has
the most wonderful curling tailfeathers, and a
heavenly blue comes into the hue of the feathers.

VAN DOREN

Does he have a colored head too?

MACLEISH

Yes, and he has a little crest.

VAN DOREN

I've probably seen one; but offhand I don't remember.

MACLEISH

I'm sure you have.

*Knee-deep in the shallows, he dives and swims
out again to the center of the pond. He turns,
and swims to shore, using a crawl stroke. He*

273

climbs up on the bank, and dries himself with a towel.

MacLeish

It really looks like a pond in deep woods, doesn't it?

Van Doren

Yes. A little lake that you'd find in the wilderness.

MacLeish

When ducks and geese are migrating they come in here a great deal.

Van Doren

Of course.

MacLeish

Wheel, and come in.

Van Doren

They suddenly see it. They say oh, oh!

MacLeish

They suddenly see it.

Van Doren lays the back of his hand on Mac-Leish's shoulder.

Van Doren

You feel nice and cool.

274

MacLeish

You ought to try it, boy. It's just a lovely temperature.

Van Doren

From the feel of it, it must be close to 70°.

MacLeish

Yes, about that. You know, Mark, it's sad about all those leaning birches; they'll never straighten up again. Or will they? Do you think they will?

Van Doren

Not much, I'm afraid.

Frog

Garumph.

MacLeish

Another one of your friends is talking to you.

Van Doren

I hear.

MacLeish

I think they must answer each other.

Van Doren

And each one of those sounds may mean something.

275

MacLeish

Such as, "Look out for that gray-haired bastard over there on the dam." (*They laugh.*)

Van Doren

It would be interesting to see if those birches do rise. That one over there was probably caught in the ice. It's already free to the extent that the ice has let go. Maybe it'll keep on going up.

MacLeish

It may go up.

Van Doren

You know, Archie, when you first swam out there, some little birds came to investigate you, but they didn't do it this time.

MacLeish

What did they say?

Van Doren

They just skimmed along and decided, "That's a man." And they didn't come back the second time. They're watching you from the woods.

MacLeish

Barn swallows?

Van Doren

I don't know what they were. They might have been swallows.

MacLeish (*finishes drying himself*)
Well, I feel cooler. I wish you did, my friend.

Van Doren
I feel cooler for you. Archie, look at that hemlock tree up there. Isn't that a lovely thing?

MacLeish
Yes, and there are quite a lot of beeches around here too. We don't get beeches anywhere else. That's a beech, and there are some beeches down there on the side.

Van Doren
The ash tree is a lovely thing, a young ash. So straight. You know, Archie, this day has turned out to be very sweetening.

MacLeish
Yes, it has. (*They stand silently together. A time passes and then:*) You know, Mark, one thing we didn't talk about, and perhaps wisely didn't —you spoke of Wordsworth as your first master, when you were reading, that is, the man who attracted you. But if you looked over the whole area of your life, and considered who it was that had most influenced you—I'm not talking now about poetry, I'm talking about the whole course of your life—could you answer that question? I don't think I could.

277

VAN DOREN

No, I can't either, and I was hoping you wouldn't put it to me directly.

MACLEISH

I don't think anybody can answer that question. And yet when I was talking about "B" Hand earlier today—and "B" Hand is certainly a man —I wondered if "B" ever influenced me. I don't know that I consciously undertook to adopt any view of his or opinion of his, and yet, he was a very great sort of confirming and supporting influence.

VAN DOREN

Oh yes.

MACLEISH

It's a strange thing when you think about it. One is formed by all sorts of contacts, relationships— your wife, your friends.

VAN DOREN (*grinning*)

You've had me, of course.

MACLEISH

I think it's very rarely that a man is really shaped or given a new direction by a given individual. I think you, probably, have yourself given direction to individuals throughout your life.

VAN DOREN

I almost hope not, as a matter of fact.

MACLEISH

Yes, one does hope not.

VAN DOREN

You know what I mean by that?

MACLEISH

Yes, I do. I do.

VAN DOREN

I'd rather think that a certain number of persons had found out more about themselves with my help.

MACLEISH

That puts it awfully well, yes.

VAN DOREN

That's about all you can ever do, is help a person to discover himself. You know, when you're asked for advice, oftentimes all you've really been asked to do is to help a person find out what he thinks.

MACLEISH

Yes.

VAN DOREN

He doesn't quite know. But in talking to you he may discover it.

MacLeish

> If you know the way in which to ask the question which will help him to discover it.

Van Doren

> That's right. You talk to him in such a way that you don't get in his way. You show how much you are interested in him.

MacLeish

> Well, Mark, are you ready to go back? Let's continue over the green world.

Van Doren

> Yes, that's a good idea, Archie. Let's go.

> *MacLeish dresses, and then he and Van Doren start back along the path through the woods to the house on the hill.*

NOTES ⇒ ⇒ ⇒

Part One

PAGE

22 University of Illinois, 1913.

26 Robert Frost in his speech at a dinner given by Amherst College, on the occasion of his eightieth birthday, March 26, 1954.

27 *Illinois Magazine,* 1914; a student publication of the University of Illinois.

29 Used by T. S. Eliot in his essay on Keats' "Ode on a Grecian Urn"; originally from Shakespeare's *King Lear,* Act V, Scene 2, Line 9.

30 "The Two Trees" from *Act Five and Other Poems* by Archibald MacLeish; Random House, 1948.

34 Herbert Sebastian Agar, American author and publisher; *The People's Choice,* 1935 (won Pulitzer Prize for American History); *A Time for Greatness,* 1942; *The Price of Power,* 1957, among others. Resides in England.

36 "The Black Day," by Archibald MacLeish, appeared in the *New York Herald Tribune* on December 24, 1948. Laurence H. Duggan: a former director of the Office of American Republics, was allegedly associated with Whittaker Chambers. It has never been established whether Duggan's death in 1948 was accidental or suicidal. Following his death Duggan was

281

cleared of espionage charges by the House Un-American Activities Committee.

39 Robert Ardrey, *African Genesis;* Atheneum, 1961.

41 Percy Bysshe Shelley (1792–1822); "Music, When Soft Voices Die," written in 1821, published by Mrs. Shelley, *Posthumous Poems,* 1824.

43 John Keats (1795–1821); "Ode to a Nightingale," written in May, 1819, first published in *Annals of the Fine Arts,* July, 1819.

60 "Under This Building" from *Collected and New Poems, 1924–1963* by Mark Van Doren; Hill and Wang, 1963.

72 Whittaker Chambers (1901–61); a former senior editor of *Life* magazine and author of *Witness,* 1952; a principal witness in the Alger Hiss trials of 1948 and 1949.

72 Lionel Trilling, author and Professor of English at Columbia University; *Matthew Arnold,* 1939; *A Gathering of Fugitives,* 1956, among others.

74 Mark Van Doren was Literary Editor of *The Nation* from 1924 to 1928.

77 Boylston Professorship of Rhetoric and Oratory: the oldest chair in the Department of English at Harvard University, first held by John Quincy Adams.

85 Dorothy Graffe Van Doren, married Mark in 1922.

89 Commenting on the object of poetry as truth, Wordsworth wrote ". . . carried alive into the heart by passion" in the preface to *Lyrical Ballads,* first published in 1800.

93   "Beauty is truth, truth beauty,—that is all
        Ye know on earth, and all ye need to know."
"Ode on a Grecian Urn" by John Keats, written in 1819, first published in *Annals of the Fine Arts,* no. XV, January, 1820.

95 The correct version is: "Fellow citizens, we cannot escape history."

97 The correct version is: ". . . The fiery trial through which we pass will light us down, in honor or dishonor, to the last generation. . . . We shall nobly save or meanly lose the last, best hope of earth."

102   John Jay Chapman (1862–1933), attorney and author; *Emerson and Other Essays,* 1898; *Dante,* 1927, among others.

103   *JB* by Archibald MacLeish, produced in December, 1958; won Pulitzer Prize for Theater in 1958–59 season.

106   *The Last Days of Lincoln* by Mark Van Doren, 1959; published by Hill and Wang, 1959, and produced at Florida State University, October, 1961.

111   Emily Dickinson (1830–86), poet. Only two of her poems were published during her lifetime. The first edition of her works was *Poems,* 1890. A three-volume edition of her work, edited by T. H. Johnson, was published in 1955.

117   Religious body first known as the United Society of Believers originated in England around 1706 as an outgrowth of the Quaker Society. Ann Lee, "Mother Ann," became their leader in 1758, brought them to the United States and organized a society at Watervliet, New York; in 1963 there were less than fifty Shakers living.

117   Bay of Pigs Invasion, April 17, 1961. American-backed Cuban exiles landed in Cuba in an abortive attempt to overthrow the Castro government.

128   "The Trenchants" by Mark Van Doren, completed in 1961; unpublished.

146   Allen Tate, critic and poet; awarded Bollingen Prize in Poetry in 1956. Author of *The Hovering Fly,* 1949; *Collected Essays,* 1960, among others.

146   Malcolm Cowley, author; *Exile's Return,* 1934, revised 1951; *Writers at Work,* 1958, among others.

147   Joseph Wood Krutch, author and critic; Professor of English at Columbia University 1937–43 and Columbia University Brander Matthews Professor of Dramatic Literature 1943–52. *The Measure of Man,* 1954 (National Book Award); *The Voice of the Desert,* 1955, among others.

148   John Crowe Ransom, poet and university professor. Bollingen Prize in Poetry, 1951; National Book Award for Poetry, 1964. *Poems About God,* 1919; *Selected Poems,* 1945; *The New Criticism,* 1941, among others.

151 Charles Percy Snow, English novelist and scientist. Author of *Two Cultures and the Scientific Revolution* (1959) and the sequence of novels, *Strangers and Brothers.*

152 Polykarp Kusch, Professor of Physics at Columbia University; conducts original research in atomic, molecular and nuclear physics; recipient of Nobel Prize for Physics, 1955.

153 Robert Oppenheimer, physicist, Director and Professor of Physics, Institute for Advanced Study, Princeton, since 1947; recipient of the Atomic Commission's Enrico Fermi award, 1963.

Part Two

PAGE

183 Ada Hitchcock and Archibald MacLeish were married in 1916.

199 George Seferis, pen name of Giorgos Stylianou Seferiades, poet and diplomat. Winner of the 1963 Nobel Prize in Literature. His collected poems were reprinted in *Poems,* Little, Brown, 1961.

215 *The People, Yes* by Carl Sandburg, published in 1936 by Harcourt, Brace.

220 Following the U.S. Steel Corporation's announcement on April 10, 1962, of an increase in prices, President John F. Kennedy, in a press conference, called this "a wholly unjustifiable and irresponsible defiance of the public interest." Kennedy threatened reprisals through the FTC and Department of Justice. As a result the steel companies rescinded their announcement of steel price increases, and some criticism was leveled at Administration tactics pertaining to the entire affair. ". . . the opponents of competitive enterprise have grown immensely powerful. With flagrant disregard for facts, they can now denounce, discredit and vilify business leaders before the public . . . and have their assault spearheaded by the highest office in the land. . . ."

242 Mark Van Doren's oldest brother (1885–1950): *Benjamin Franklin;* an autobiography, *Three Worlds,* and others.

284

251 Thomas Merton, priest, ordained in 1949, and now the Master of Novices at Abbey of Gethsemane. Author and poet; *Seven Storey Mountain*, 1948; *No Man Is an Island*, 1955; *Selected Poems*, 1959, among others.

253 "Jewish Students I Have Known," *Menorah Journal*, 1927.

255 Nellie Foster, friend and housekeeper.

ACKNOWLEDGMENTS ⇒ ⇒ ⇒

Murray Benson first believed "The Dialogues" could be —should be published as a book.

Archie and Mark said it was all right—with slightly raised eyebrows.

Jack Kiermaier allowed as how it would be okay—if it could be worked in.

Maryse Addison was the journeyman—trenchantly.

P.A.T. helped in untold ways.

The pink conch-girl eavesdropped—amicably.

And Ada MacLeish graciously forgave me for placing my cigarette in her salad dish.

W.V.B.